Federalism and the British

Federalism and The British

edited by Stanley Henig

The Federal Trust

This book is published by the Federal Trust whose aim is to enlighten public debate on issues arising from the interaction of national, European and global levels of government. It does this in the light of its statutes which state that it shall promote 'studies in the principles of international relations, international justice and supranational government.'

Up-to-date information about the Federal Trust can be found on the internet at: http://www.fedtrust.co.uk

© Federal Trust for Education and Research 2007
ISBN 1 903403 88 4

The Federal Trust is a Registered Charity No. 272241
7 Graphite Square, Vauxhall Walk,
London SE11 5EE
Company Limited by Guarantee No. 1269848

Designed by Anthony Cohen
Printed in the European Union

Contents

Foreword

Federalism and The British

The bulk of this book is devoted to presenting, in revised and slightly modified form, a series of papers presented to a conference at the Centre for Federal Studies, University of Kent, with the support of the James Madison Trust in July 2006. The object of the James Madison Trust is to support research into the many aspects of federalism. It has, over the last few years, supported a number of conferences bringing together academics, writers, politicians and campaigners. This current volume, arising from the Kent conference, reflects the diversity of their contributions and is intended to offer an overview of the contributions made by British thinkers, writers and practitioners to the development of federal thinking and the impact of those contributions on political thought both within and outside the United Kingdom.

SH

Introduction

Britain's Love/Hate Relationship with Federalism

Stanley Henig

IT WOULD BE A GROSS UNDERSTATEMENT TO SUGGEST that in recent years "federalism" has not enjoyed a good press in Britain! What is curious is that federalism in both theory and practice was in large part conceived by British political thinkers. Our norm with what we think of as British inventions or innovations is to bemoan the way in which others have taken them over, claimed credit for their existence or, perhaps, traduced them in some way: from the world of sport we can cite both soccer and rugby; in governance the concepts of constitutional monarchy and cabinet government. It is quite different with "federalism." The key role of British political philosophers in developing federal thinking along with our bequeathing federal-type constitutions to many Commonwealth countries as well as the British contribution towards constructing the post Second World War constitution of the Federal Republic of Germany have seemingly been expunged from the public memory. Indeed, not content with implying all too often that "federalism" itself is somehow alien to Britain and Britishness, the media have gone on to invent something labelled a "federal superstate." Such a concept is totally without meaning – by definition a federal state can only be the complete opposite of the superstate. Indeed, at the very heart of federalism lies the concept of division of power – especially between different tiers of government – with clear, constitutionally defined limits placed on the power and scope of the central authority or any institution within that authority.

This is the context within which the Federal Trust is publishing the current volume – its chapters originally contributed as papers at a conference organised at the Centre for Federal Studies, University of Kent, with the support of the James Madison Trust. The overarching theme of the book is the development and spread of federal ideas and, specifically, the role of British thinkers, politicians and others in that process. Our historic span –

indeed a journey - covers more than two centuries. It begins with Maurice Vile showing how the American colonies were in a sense reacting against what could be construed as transient efforts by the British government to act in colonial affairs as if it were indeed a kind of superstate. This chapter sketches the contribution made by British thinkers to the gradual establishment of the US as the world's first state to be structured along federal and democratic lines. Even at the end of our time span the journey is by no means over. Britain is now an integral part of the European Union. In the latter part of the final chapter of the book, John Pinder discusses ways in which our own national interests and preoccupations, above all in the international sphere, can best be met through the conferment of additional federal elements to the Union's institutions and competences.

Reverting to the first part of the book, Michael Burgess traces the development of federal thinking in Britain, drawing particular attention to ways in which thinkers, writers and active politicians saw federalism as a means of tackling specific constitutional and political problems. Some were internal to the United Kingdom – particularly with regard to relations between its constituent parts. Others concerned Empire and Commonwealth – relations between different countries and the constitutions bequeathed to newly independent states. There were two occasions when federalism made a major impact on the political process and the controversies of the day. The first was during and towards the end of the imbroglio leading to Irish home rule – politicians, civil servants and others in public life argued for a federal solution which might reinforce the United Kingdom - and they did gain media support. The second was the nearest federalism came to becoming a popular cause in Britain. In the run up to the Second World War Federal Union was, albeit briefly, a significant political player. In this context Burgess reminds us of Churchill's thirteenth hour proposal for a federal union between Britain and France. After the war Britain played a leading role in helping to draft the constitution for the Federal Republic of Germany.

Lucio Levi's paper returns to, and revolves around, the theme of the international spread of ideas: particularly the impact of British federal thinking on Italian federalists, above all Altiero Spinelli, during the later wartime years of his incarceration under Mussolini. Forty years on, Spinelli, still imbued with ideas learned from British federalists, would be a driving force in the conversion of the European Community into the European Union.

The prism through which federalism is viewed in these early chapters is a series of major world events – the American revolution, the relationship between different parts of the United Kingdom, the evolution of Empire, the impact of the Second World War and the beginnings of European integration. However, their perspective is largely theoretical – the overarching theme is the spread of federal ideas. Ernest Wistrich introduces a quite different note by focusing on federalists as active politicians - taking the lead in a series of political campaigns, for British entry into the European Community and, subsequently and equally successfully, against proposals to withdraw from membership.

In the real world our physical membership of the European Community and, now, the European Union may not be in doubt. The degree of commitment is another question. Richard Corbett traces the evolution of party attitudes towards Community and Union. At different times all three main political parties have supported measures leading to further integration and, implicitly therefore, towards federalism. But, because of the success of the media campaign against the concept, a sense of denial is pervasive. Inching forward whilst looking backward is hardly an elegant posture! It could, of course, be the basis for a leap forward rather than another tiny step. John Palmer points to the current problems affecting our own parliamentary democracy. He argues persuasively for pan-European parties concerned with pan-European issues and making a positive contribution towards resolving our current malaise. It may be worth recalling in this context that when British membership of the EC was first mooted there was a general view that in terms of domestic political institutions we had little to learn from Europe.

The dreaded "f" initial recurs throughout this book – shorthand for federalism. Brendan Donnelly uses the letter to introduce another word: "fear" – "nothing to fear but fear itself." The entire thrust of Britain's European policy over the last 60 years has been motivated by fear – fear of being left out balancing fear of involvement. Can we now stop being frightened and envisage Europe as part of our normal political landscape: a forum and a basis for developing new policies containing a specific British interest? This helps set the scene for the last chapter by John Pinder, summarising the historic development of federal thinking and the successive stages in the construction to date of a European federal entity, and suggesting that the process could be given a considerable further impulse through a major enhancement of the European Union's external capacity. Passim he shows how Britain has been involved in previous stages of that construction and how the proposed completion would be in accordance with our own national interests.

The above chapters were originally conceived as working papers for a conference about institutions and ideas. But it is always worth remembering that events and ideas ultimately revolve around the contributions of individuals. Lucio Levi's chapter outlines the intellectual origins of Spinelli's commitment and contribution to the concept of the European Union. The intellectual father of its precursor, the European Community, was Jean Monnet. Richard Mayne worked with him over many years and offers an authoritative assessment of his role and contribution. This was presented at the conference as an after-dinner speech; the style has been retained for this book for which it seemed appropriate to juxtapose Mayne's "envoi" with Levi's chapter at the end of Part one. What percolates Mayne's "envoi" is Monnet's passionate belief in Britain and his sense of what was "Britishness." He was totally committed to our being part of the Europe in the construction of which he was so influential.

Those three substantive chapters at the beginning of this book – by Vile, Burgess and Levi – trace the way in which federal thinking has evolved over recent centuries. However, certain core ideas are broadly unchanged. I want to complete this brief introductory chapter with a few reflections on these ideas positioned at the centre of federal thinking and thus constituting the essence of federalism. I suggested in the first paragraph that the division of powers – especially between different tiers of government – lies at the heart of federalism. Clear constitutionally defined limits are placed on the power and scope of central authority or any institution within the area governed by that authority. In pursuance of this line of thinking it is possible to go rather further: the powers and competences of two or more tiers of governmental institutions are similarly defined. Moreover, the definitions of, and limitations to, powers and competences have to be set out in a formal constitution. It is important in this context to recognise that pluralism and federalism are not the same. Pluralism does indeed imply limitations on government power and authority. Those limitations can arise in a number of ways, including through the media and economic interest groups. The limitations may be more or less effective, but in a real sense they are conditioned and operated through market forces. Federalism goes beyond pluralism in not simply relying on market forces. Indeed this perhaps helps to explain historically the attraction of federal ideas for some socialists, particularly in the period immediately before 1939. When it comes to organising our political and economic structures, the mechanisms of the so-called free market may seem to some to be equally inadequate.

In turn we can point to certain specifics which must be included if the constitutional law is to have a federal nature. First and foremost the existence of the separate tiers of governance and their basic powers cannot be altered unilaterally by either tier or by any one authority. The constitution can be amended, but the process must involve both tiers of governance. It also follows that "ownership of the constitution" or sovereignty must ultimately be vested in the whole of the population. Two considerations seem to me to follow. The first is that the institutions at each tier of governance must be legitimated through direct elections. The second is that the concepts of parliamentary sovereignty – Westminster style – and federalism are, in the final analysis, incompatible. Parliamentary sovereignty implies that no parliament can bind its successors. Theoretically a recipe allowing for change and modernisation, this means in practice that the Westminster Parliament is at all times in a position to alter both constitutional law and constitutional lore. In such a regime it is impossible to entrench the existence and powers of other tiers of government.

Secondly, if constitutional law is to have a federal nature, there is another almost equally important requirement. Each tier of governance and each separate government within the lower tier must have a guaranteed source of income, which cannot simply be turned off by other tiers or other authorities. Financial autonomy is an essential feature of a federal constitution.

There is one further consideration before entering the substance of this book. Federalism and federation are not the same. A federation is a comprehensive structure and system of government by definition devised along federal principles. However, federal thinking can permeate any governmental system to a greater or lesser extent. Thus federal ideas may co-exist with centralised or unitary states and devolved structures within them. In Western Europe Germany is a federation and, by most criteria, Belgium is also in that category. France, Italy, Spain and the United Kingdom are not federations. But federal thinking is present in different ways in their respective constitutional arrangements – even in the United Kingdom where, in theory at least, no national parliament can bind its successors. All six of the countries mentioned in this paragraph are part of a European Union, in considerable part constructed in accordance with federal principles. The state of denial analysed in the chapters by Corbett, Palmer and Donnelly is hardly a recipe for a healthy polity at any level. The prime objectives of this book are to challenge that state of denial and to explain what federalism is – particularly in the European context.

Finally, and almost by way of a postscript: the conference which produced the papers in this book was to a considerable extent over-shadowed by discussions as to Europe's future constitutional arrangements following the French and Dutch referendums. The Constitutional Treaty – approved by many member states, rejected by France and the Netherlands and side-stepped by the United Kingdom – can be seen as a way of ensuring more effective and democratic decision making processes, particularly in the light of the considerable expansion of EU membership. The reality – implicitly underlined throughout this book – is that the European Community and the European Union have always had a 'constitution'. No organisation of its size and scope could operate without one. However, like the British constitution that of the European Union has always been un-codified – in part written statute and in part unwritten convention. It is inevitable that the balance between these two parts will change in time, but it is no part of the purpose of this book to discuss the extent to which the replacement 'Reform Treaty' mirrors the 'Constitutional Treaty'.

Part One

The British Contribution to the Federal Idea from the Eighteenth to the Twentieth Century

Britain has played a major role in the evolution of federal thinking over more than two centuries. Many of the ideas underpinning the constitution of the US were drawn from British political theory and practice. The trajectory and historical development of the constitutional and political history of the US and the UK may seem markedly different, but in different ways federal thinking has permeated both. Federal models were explored for handling both relationships between the constituent parts of the United Kingdom and between the latter and its overseas empire. In considerable part the emerging federal system of the European Community and European Union has been the inspiration of two men – Jean Monnet and Altiero Spinelli. Monnet was profoundly influenced by British pragmatism; Spinelli for his part drew much of his inspiration from British federal thinkers.

Chapter 1

British Influences on the American Founding Fathers: Lessons for Europe

Maurice Vile

THE FOUNDING OF THE AMERICAN REPUBLIC PROVIDES A FASCINATING PICTURE of the evolution of British ideas on federalism and the relevance they might have for the future constitution of Europe. To approach this problem we will need to do two things: first, to take a more realistic view of the American Founding Fathers than is often offered in the eulogies that claim to portray the creation of the constitution of the United States; second, to offer a more constructive view of federalism as a pattern for the future structure of Europe than is usually evident in the yah-boo style of everyday British politics.

The Founding Fathers

To begin with, a very obvious but important point: the colonists at the time of the Constitutional Convention were overwhelmingly British or Irish. In the mid-1770s there was no real distinction between being American and being British. In 1790 between 60 and 80 per cent of the population of the United States was English or Welsh in origin, 14 per cent were of Scottish or Irish stock; Germans made up the only other significant group. The importance of this fact in the construction of the new constitutional order can hardly be exaggerated. Thomas Jefferson's A Summary View of the Rights of British America written in July 1774 is a magnificent example of the motivations of the revolutionaries and the ideas they used to justify their actions. The document was penned as an "instruction" to the Virginian deputies to the Continental Congress "when assembled in general congress with the deputies from the other states of British America, to propose to the said congress that an humble and dutiful address be presented to his majesty, begging leave to lay before him, as chief magistrate of the British empire, the united complaints of his majesty's subjects in America." The Summary View is a remarkable mish-mash of arguments, setting out the colonies' grievances against the British Crown and Parliament, justifying rebellion, asking for reconciliation, appealing alternately to the traditional rights of British subjects, to the natural rights of man, or to the structure of an ancient British constitution which had never existed.

The motives of the rebellious colonists are revealing. Of course the revolution was in large part the result of the actions of a stupid monarch and a parliament insensitive to the realities of the politics of dealing with colonies at a great distance from the mother country, colonies which had enjoyed considerable independence in the conduct of their affairs for over one hundred years before the British government attempted to assert greater control over colonial trade, government and taxation. The colonies had genuine grievances, which were recognised by the merchants of London who petitioned the House of Commons in 1774 asking for the repeal of the Acts which were disrupting the traditional trade relations between Britain and her colonies. However, the rhetoric of oppression, subjection, slavery even, employed by the more radical opponents of British power such as Patrick Henry, masks the real nature of the problem. Even Jefferson, in the Summary View, can descend to almost farcical claims: "By an act passed in the 5th Year of the reign of his late majesty king George the second, an American subject is forbidden to make a hat for himself of the fur which he has taken perhaps on his own soil; an instance of despotism to which no parallel can be produced in the most arbitrary ages of British history." In fact the American colonists in the eighteenth century enjoyed more liberty than any other people on the planet; certainly more than the majority of the citizens of Britain itself.

What then were the reasons why the American Revolution occurred when it did? An insensitive and incompetent government in England was a major factor. But if the demand for independence had not arisen under George III and Lord North, it would have happened sooner or later. The colonists wished to be in charge of their own destinies. They were prepared to accept nominal British rule, provided that they were allowed to determine their own fate. They were idealists in respect of liberty and freedom, but they were above all realists, who recognised their own interests and were determined to pursue them. The defeat of the French and their Indian allies by the British army under General Wolfe at Quebec in 1759 removed the major threat to the American colonies which had required the protection of the British army. The Proclamation of 1763, which reserved the lands to the west of the Appalachians to the Crown, threatened the anticipated expansion of Virginia and other colonies into the vast expanses of western lands extending to the Pacific Ocean, to which they laid claim. The original charters of Virginia, Pennsylvania and Massachusetts had given them rights all the way to the Pacific; Madison, Jefferson and others thought of the future extension of a western empire.[1] Jefferson, Madison and other Founders were land speculators, hoping to make considerable profits from westward expansion.[2] The control of the Mississippi Valley and the danger of losing that control to France or Spain were crucial to the future of Anglo-America. The colonists were not prepared to see their potential gains subverted by the British government.

Another way of looking at the American Revolution is to see it as a rerun of the English Civil War.[3] The Civil War had significant consequences for the American colonies. It loosened the ties between Britain and the colonists, most of whom were more sympathetic to Cromwell than to Charles I. It made the colonists more self-reliant, and accelerated the tendency towards popular sovereignty in America. The religious dimension of the American Revolution also mirrored that of the English Civil War. Puritanism, Presbyterianism and Quakerism were the dominant religious movements in a number of the colonies, and there was resistance to having bishops sent from England even in Anglican Virginia.

Perhaps more important than any of these considerations was the natural development of the attitudes of British colonists who wished to control their own affairs. In settler societies such as the American colonies, the initial stage of dependence on the mother country for support against indigenous peoples, for protection against other colonial powers, for essential supplies of domestic animals, manufactured goods and luxury items, comes to an end when security is assured, when domestic agriculture and industry have been established, and when social structures are stable enough for self-government to operate. At this stage co-operation or even competition characterises the relationship between the colony and the imperial power. When co-operation breaks down, or when the settlers feel that they can better realise their ambitions by making their own decisions over domestic and even foreign policies, demands for independence begin to be made. In this respect American independence was inevitable, whatever the response of the British government in the 1770s had been; the only issue was the timing of this demand. The incompetence of the British government of the time only speeded up the process. Similar developments were later to take place in Canada, Australia and New Zealand, but fortunately the lessons of the American Revolution had been learnt and, sometimes with considerable difficulty, the former colonies emerged as Dominions and then as independent states, without the need for revolution.

Above all then the Founding Fathers were realists. They no doubt believed the rhetoric of the Declaration of Independence, but they were following their interests as they saw them. They were not demi-gods; they were "human, all too human" in the words of historian Bruce Ackerman.[4] The importance to them of unfettered westward expansion cannot be exaggerated, and the nineteenth century became the era of expansion from the Louisiana Purchase of 1803, the Indian Wars, the annexation of Texas, the Mexican-American War, to the annexation of Hawaii in 1898. Americans were opposed to imperialism except when it came to their own claim to the continent of North America, founded on the claims first made in the name of Queen Elizabeth I.

The Founders were also realists when it came to the question of slavery. Madison and others opposed slavery but in practice were prepared to tolerate it, because they considered it necessary for the foundation of the union to do so. Charles Cotesworth Pinckney, a member of the Federal Convention from South Carolina, returned to his home state saying: "By this settlement, we have secured an unlimited importation of Negroes for twenty years... we have a right to recover our slaves in whatever part of America they may take refuge... considering all the circumstances, we have made the best terms for the security of this species of property it was in our power to make."[5]

Realism also triumphed over idealism in relation to the attitudes of the revolutionaries towards the alliance with France. Madison and others were very happy to accept the alliance with France, and indeed with Spain, because of the necessity for military support in order to defeat the British. Indeed, the strategy was successful. There were more French soldiers at the Battle of Yorktown in 1781 than there were British soldiers, and the French navy played an important role in preventing the reinforcement of the British army. But these were the soldiers and sailors of Louis XVI, the most authoritarian ruler in Europe, whose subjects were denied even the most basic human rights. The devotion of some of the American revolutionaries to the French monarchy went even further. In Philadelphia in 1782 Madison and others mounted a magnificent celebration to mark the birth of the Dauphin to Marie Antoinette. La Luzerne, the French minister, built a pavilion to house 600 dinner guests.[6]

The Founders of the United States were concerned primarily, as are most politicians, with the furtherance of their "national" interest, and were prepared, within limits, to do whatever was necessary to that end. They drew upon British sources for their political theories, and upon British history to fashion their institutions. This was true also in the formation of the new federal union. The Founding Fathers had studied the ancient confederacies, and they knew about the United Netherlands, but none of these really offered a blueprint for the solution of the problem that faced them – how to unite 13 disparate colonies, each of which was proud of its own traditions, and each of which had a distinctive economic and social makeup. But there were materials ready to hand from their own history.

The British theory of mixed and balanced government – a mix of monarchy, aristocracy and democracy embodied in King, Lords and Commons – with its roots in antiquity, had been elaborated by Sir John Fortescue in the mid-sixteenth century and had been at the centre of the seventeenth-century conflict between King and Parliament. It was embodied in the Bill of Rights of 1689 and became in the eighteenth century the Whig theory of the British Constitution. Madison and other Founding Fathers described themselves as "American Whigs."[7] The Glorious Revolution was their inspiration. Although they had to adapt the theory to a political system without king or hereditary aristocracy, the mixed and balanced constitution was always at the centre of their thoughts.

The second central concept of American constitutionalism – the theory of the separation of powers – was derived from English political thought at the time of the Civil War. The doctrine of the separation of powers in its modern form originates in the thoughts of the opponents of royal power in mid-seventeenth century England and in their efforts to construct a constitution for a commonwealth, not from the Frenchman, Montesquieu, as is so often asserted.[8] Thus the American Constitution, written in 1787, mirrored the structure of the Cromwellian Constitution, the *Instrument of Government* of 1653. Article I of the *Instrument* vested the supreme legislative authority in a Lord Protector and the people assembled in Parliament, but the role of the Lord Protector was limited to a suspensive veto of 20 days. If after that period the Lord Protector "hath not consented nor given satisfaction" then on a declaration of parliament the bill became law without his consent, the forerunner of the presidential veto power in the American Constitution. Article II of the *Instrument* provided that "the exercise of the chief magistracy, and the administration of the government... shall be in the Lord Protector, assisted with a council." Marchamont Nedham, the apologist for the *Instrument*, set out the theory of the separation of powers that was later to form the basis of the American Constitution. In *A True State of the Case for the Commonwealth* of 1654 he argued that "placing the legislative and executive powers in the same persons, is a marvellous inlet of corruption and tyranny." Even worse if these powers were joined in the hands of an assembly "for such a multitude can more easily escape responsibility."[9] There was much fellow feeling for the parliamentary cause in America; a group of regicides were given refuge in Hadley, Massachusetts. John Adams stated that Nedham's work was well known in colonial America and the behaviour of the revolutionary state legislatures after 1776 confirmed the fears expressed by Nedham of the abuse of power by the legislature. The American Revolution was a reaffirmation of the right of the representatives of the people to oppose the exercise of arbitrary royal power, and the Constitution of 1789 was the embodiment and elaboration of English political thought.

The Founding Fathers drew their inspiration from British sources, above all from John Locke. *The Two Treatises on Government* published in 1690 offered a justification of the Revolution of 1688-9 based upon natural rights and natural law. Natural law, a claim to innate, indefeasible rights inherent in every individual, including the right to property, led to the idea that the community was limited in its competence to interfere with the liberty and property of the individual. There was no real justification given for this belief by Locke; he assumed, as did Thomas Jefferson, that it was self-evident. The idea of the social contract, elaborated by Locke, based upon consent and respect for the concept of the Rule of Law, formed the basis of American thought and still does today. The "Glorious Revolution" was the true embodiment of the mixed and balanced constitution that had been usurped by George III and his ministers, and the English Bill of Rights of 1689, still considered operative in America, was the basis for the Bill of Rights which Madison steered through the first Congress. However, the English Bill of Rights was directed solely against executive power, whereas in America it was deemed necessary to put checks also on the powers of the legislature, and upon the popular majority of the people that might oppress the minority. Although Locke's thought did not make a direct contribution to the federal structure embodied in the Constitution (his use of the term "federative power" described the power over foreign relations), his concept of the social contract was at the core of the compact between the states.

David Hume effectively destroyed, in philosophical terms, the natural rights theory of Locke, and indeed the idea of a social contract [10], but although Hume's work was well known in America, he did not destroy the practical importance of the Lockean theory. As a philosopher perhaps his scepticism and empiricism helped to destroy any sense of the inevitability of the monarchy or of the empire. Hume's attitude to religion would not have gone down well with the Presbyterian teachers who played such an important role in Madison's life. However, Hume's *Idea of a Perfect Commonwealth*, 1741-2, a description of a federation of counties based upon Harrington's *Oceana*, may have provided the argument for Madison's *Federalist No. 10* that a wider community could be more democratic than a smaller. Hume rejected the view that "no large state... could ever be modelled into a commonwealth but that such a form of government can only take place within a city or small territory. The contrary seems probable. Though it is more difficult to form a republican government in an extensive country than in a city, there is more facility when once it is formed, of preserving it steady and uniform, without tumult and faction."[11]

Although Montesquieu was widely read and quoted in colonial America his chapter on the English Constitution was rather muddled.[12] Sir William Blackstone's *Commentaries on the Laws of England*, 1765-9, was the channel through which Montesquieu's work was transmitted to America and domesticated. Blackstone had a much clearer idea of the role of the judges than Montesquieu. The latter got the English courts mixed up with the role of the *parlements* in France. Blackstone roundly used the term "the judicial power," whereas Montesquieu had simply used *"le pouvoir de juger."* For Blackstone the courts were "the grand depositories of the fundamental laws of the kingdom," and judicial independence the cornerstone of the Constitution. It is said that the *Commentaries* were in every lawyer's office in America. The power of the Supreme Court of the United States, and its great Chief Justice, John Marshall, owed more to Blackstone than to Montesquieu.[13]

In fact, the role of the courts in pronouncing the law, the common law of England, was one of the most formative influences on the development of constitutional thought in America. Founded at a time when law was principally to be found in the decisions of courts rather than in statutes, the common law was received in the American colonies, and was seen as "a set of fundamental principles of public law that placed limitations on government and hence were constitutional in nature."[14] Sir Edward Coke, appointed as Chief Justice of the Court of Common Pleas in 1610, became the defender of the supremacy of the common law against the Stuart assertion of the royal prerogative, and his judgment in *Dr. Bonham's Case*, in which he pronounced that "when an act of parliament is against common right and reason, or repugnant, or impossible to be performed, the common law will controul it, and adjudge such act void," was used in a somewhat overstated way by James Otis in 1761 in Massachusetts to argue that Acts of Parliament which violated fundamental law were void.[15] In 1803, Chief Justice John Marshall in the case of *Marbury v. Madison*, the first case in which an Act of Congress was declared unconstitutional, whilst not mentioning Coke by name, used the same words "void" and "repugnant" that Coke had employed nearly 200 years earlier.[16]

Federalism

The third leg of the constitution constructed by the Convention in 1787 – federalism – is not so clearly derived from English, or British, political theory, but it emerged naturally from the experience of the colonies as part of the British Empire. The colonial constitutions embodied the theory of mixed government, including elected assemblies: a degree of democracy to be found in no other empire of the time. In 1621 the Ordinance for the Government of Virginia established a royal governor, a Council of State including 20 local worthies and a General Assembly consisting of two burgesses from every town, hundred or plantation "to be chosen by the inhabitants." The Ordinance declared: "All matter shall be decided, determined, and ordered by the greater part of the voices then present; reserving always to the governor a negative voice." The Ordinance set out the powers of the General Assembly: "This General Assembly shall have free power to treat, consult and conclude... of all emergent questions concerning the public weal of the said colony... as also to make, ordain and enact such general laws and orders, for the Behoof of the said colony, and the good government thereof, as shall, from time to time, appear necessary or requisite." Initially all freemen in Virginia were entitled to vote although the franchise later underwent many changes because of local political battles. Colonial governments embodied the British model of balanced government adapted to the circumstances of the colonies. The exact pattern of government varied from colony to colony, and the extent of the power exercised by royal governors over representative institutions, or their attempts to do so, changed as imperial policy changed, particularly in regard to trade. In spite of the problems which arose with Britain, the general regard for the balanced constitution continued in America, so that as late as 1772 it was being urged as the pattern of the ideal system of government which was being subverted by the actions of the British government.[17]

Thus the American colonies enjoyed a considerable degree of self-government, the extent of which depended upon their distance from the home country and the degree to which the imperial government was able or minded to control their affairs. In law the British Empire in America was not a federal system, but in terms of politics it was. The effective working of a federal system depends on two interrelated factors – a federal constitution and the federal spirit, that is the willingness to see political decisions made at more than one level of government. Attempts were made in America to develop a federal theory of the British Empire, notably by Governor Stephen Hopkins of Rhode Island and, in 1768, by John Dickinson in his *Letters from a Pennsylvania Farmer*.[18] Although the sovereignty of the imperial parliament meant that there could be no formal federal constitution, nevertheless the realities of life accustomed the colonists to the working of federal politics.

The political life and relationships of the colonies tended to be with London rather than with each other, but the formation of the Federal Constitution involved the breaking of those historical links and the creation of a union between the former colonies, now transformed into states. The idea of forming unions went back a long way. In 1643 the Confederation of New England was created. The plantations of Massachusetts, New Plymouth, Connecticut and New Haven combined into the United Colonies of New England. Two commissioners from each colony were appointed to deal with those matters, particularly defence, which were of common interest. The outbreak of the Civil War in England had made the colonies more vulnerable: "... by reason of those sad distractions in England, which they have heard of, and by which we are hindered from that humble way of seeking advice, or reaping those comfortable fruits of protection, which at other times we might well expect..."

The Articles of Confederation established that each colony should preserve entirely to itself "the peculiar jurisdiction and government" within its own limits and with these the confederation was never "to intermeddle." Each colony had equal representation. Decisions could be made by three-fourths of the delegates on all matters of war or peace. There was a president chosen from among them, but his role was to act purely as a chairman. It provided also for the return of fugitive slaves. The confederation lasted for 40 years.[19]

In the years which followed there were several other plans for the union of the colonies, from the attempt by James II to establish a Dominion of New England, up to Joseph Galloway's Plan of Union of 1774, which proposed that the Continental Congress should apply to His Majesty for a redress of the grievances under which his subjects were suffering, assuring the King that: "The colonies hold in abhorrence the idea of being considered independent communities on the British Government, and most ardently desire the establishment of a political union, not only among themselves, but with the mother state... That a British and American legislature, for regulating the administration of the general affairs of America, be proposed and established in America, including all the said colonies; within and under which government, each colony shall retain its present constitution and powers of regulating and governing its own internal police in all cases whatsoever."

The details of the plan, including the division of powers between the colonies and the Grand Council of the Union, need not detain us, for it was defeated in the Congress, although by only one vote. No doubt the leaders of the revolution were relieved that this challenge to their plans for taking control of their own affairs had evaporated. It is nonetheless interesting that, although differing in very many respects from the Constitution that emerged from the Convention 13 years later, the major elements of a British federal state in North America were set out.[20]

A further contribution of the imperial structure to the future constitution of the United States lay in the role of the Privy Council as the ultimate arbiter of the legality of the Acts of colonial legislatures. Even if legislative Acts passed by the Council and Assembly of a colony had received the assent of the colony's royal governor they could be declared invalid by the Privy Council in London, on the grounds that they conflicted with English law, and the Privy Council also acted as the judge in disputes between colonial governors and their legislative bodies. The Privy Council was composed of royal advisors and was by no means a body of professional judges; it was not until 1833 that the Judicial Committee of the Privy Council was established, consisting of professional judges, to deal, amongst other things, with constitutional and legal issues arising from the actions of colonial legislatures. In the eighteenth century such matters were dealt with by the Privy Council as a body advising the monarch on a wide range of political issues, but the combination of executive and judicial powers in one body was well understood at the time. Although the colonists were often angered by this confounding of the powers of government in one set of hands, the concept of disallowing colonial legislative Acts on the grounds that they conflicted with English law was not in itself unacceptable, at least until the revolution. In the light of this experience, the Constitutional Convention drafted the Supremacy Clause, Article VI, of the Constitution: "This Constitution, and the Laws of the United States which shall be made in Pursuance thereof... shall be the supreme Law of the Land, and the Judges in every State shall be bound thereby, any Thing in the Constitution or Laws of any State to the Contrary notwithstanding."

James Madison

James Madison, the Father of the Constitution, was a pragmatic politician, whose ability to find workable compromises saved the Constitutional Convention from deadlock. Ralph Ketchum sums him up: "Madison stood upon whatever aspect of his basic learning seemed to him relevant for the intellectual problem or political necessity at hand. His thought was eclectic, sensible, and reasonable, if not always consistent."[21] Madison had to pick his way between contending factions in the Convention. Alexander Hamilton, later Secretary of the Treasury under Washington, was an extreme centralist, stressing the importance of manufactures, commerce and financial power. The plan that he submitted to the Convention proposed that the governors of the states should be appointed by the "General Government" and should have a veto on all laws passed by the state legislature. The plan presented by William Patterson of New Jersey, however, approached the problem more from the position of a redrafting of the Articles of Confederation, the formal purpose for which the Convention had been established.

The arguments in the Convention reflected the divisions within the American elite. John Adams, a strong federalist, in his *A Defense of the Constitutions of the United States* directed his argument against radical views like those of the English defender of the Commonwealth, Marchamont Nedham. He had a pessimistic view of mankind: men were in general depraved, unfitted for government. Government should be structured in such a way as to check these tendencies. Mixed government with checks and balances on the English model, incorporating an aristocratic element, was the best system of government. The Jeffersonians on the other hand believed that the common man was basically good. Far from embracing the aristocratic notions of John Adams, Thomas Jefferson believed in the desirability of continuous revolution. At the extreme end of the Jeffersonian faction was John Taylor of Caroline County in Virginia, a friend of Madison. He had a vision of an Arcadian dream of "rural felicity." He was a strong opponent of the power of the federal government, believing that the states should govern themselves. Because all power originated in the people,

Republicans believed in the popular election of all three branches of government and that each branch should be able to develop its own interpretation of the Constitution.[22] Both sides of this debate were grounded in colonial experience and from observation of the operation of state governments after the declaration of independence, although English and French writers were used to further the arguments.

Madison urged on the Convention the necessity of a central government, which would have the power to ensure the effective defence of the United States and be able to act independently of the states in the sphere of its constitutional functions. One of the authors of the *Federalist Papers* he was a Jeffersonian, not a centralist. Secretary of State to Jefferson and elected as a Republican President in 1808, Madison wanted to steer a middle course between a highly centralised system of government and the ineffective Articles of Confederation. On the one hand, a survey of the ancient Greek confederacies showed that, because of the weakness of their central power, the constituent cities could flout the terms of the federal pact. "A weak government, when not at war, is ever agitated by internal dissensions, so these never fail to bring on fresh calamities."[23] The need was for a central authority with autonomy in the exercise of its functions; the necessity for a strong union acting directly on the people, and not through the state governments was clear. On the other hand, in the *Federalist No. 45* Madison wrote that: "The powers delegated by the proposed constitution to the federal government are few and defined. Those which are to remain in the state governments are numerous and indefinite. The former will be exercised principally on external objects... The powers reserved to the several states will extend to all the objects which in the ordinary course of affairs, concern the lives, liberties, and properties of the people...."[24]

Madison's opposition to an overbearing federal government was very plain. He drafted the Virginia Resolutions of 1798 which set out the objections of the Virginia legislature to the passage of the Alien and Sedition Acts by the Federalist Congress under the Administration of President John Adams.[25] These Resolutions, presented to the Virginia legislature by John Taylor of Caroline, affirmed: "That this Assembly doth explicitly and peremptorily declare that it views the powers of the Federal Government as resulting from the compact to which the states are parties as limited by the plain sense and intention of the instrument constructing that compact; as no further valid than they are authorized by the grants enumerated in that compact."

The Resolutions also developed some of the ideas which would eventually

Federalism and the British

lead to the demand for secession and the Civil War, particularly the doctrine of interposition, that is the right, and duty, of the states to interpose their authority between their citizens and the Federal Government when the latter exceeded its constitutional authority. Madison was clear that if the Federal Government exceeded its powers secession would be the result, although he had no wish to see this happen.[26] A more extreme version of this view was stated in the Kentucky Resolutions of 1798, drafted by Thomas Jefferson.

Thus Madison, although in favour of granting to the new Federal Government the powers necessary to the performance of its essential functions, was opposed to the extension of those powers in a way which would impinge upon the sovereignty of the states. The division of sovereignty between federal and state governments is not a concept that survives rigorous analysis by thinkers such as Jean Bodin or Hans Kelsen, but it was central to Madison's thought, and the Supreme Court of the United States still asserts this doctrine today.[27] In fact, there is a single undivided legal sovereign in the United States. It is provided for in Article V which sets out the procedure for amending the Constitution. The final legal authority consists of two-thirds of both Houses of Congress and majorities in the legislatures (or conventions) of three-fourths of the states; but this sovereign power almost never speaks. Federalism operates successfully because political power is divided, a division buttressed by the constitutional structure and delivered through the *political* process. Above all, this division of power ensures that limits are set to the operation of simple majority rule. Madison was unhappy about the idea of simple majority rule.[28] The central core of the concept of federalism is that simple majority rule is not a sufficient basis for the state.

Federal Theory and Europe
Two centuries have elapsed: today there is a pressing need for a reappraisal of British attitudes towards federalism if Britain is to play a significant part in the way in which European institutions evolve. Both sides of the political divide in Britain shy away from a realistic assessment of the nature of federalism. On one side of the argument some supporters of European integration assert that the European Union is *not* a federal state so that we need not fear that particular bogeyman; on the other side the opponents of integration proclaim that Europe is moving towards becoming a federal state and that this is a horrifying prospect and should be prevented at all costs. But the federal idea has a lot to offer to those who accept that Europe is a

reality and that it must be able to achieve its aims effectively, whilst at the same time being sceptical of the grander designs of the integrationists. Michael Burgess has pointed to the problem of attempting to define federalism and the efforts that have been made to do so.[29] There is, in fact, no Platonic idea of federalism stored up somewhere to be sought out by the philosopher, but it is possible to develop a Weberian ideal type, a model of a federal state, which can form the basis for the analysis of existing or proposed unions. In that sense, the European Union clearly possesses many characteristics that might be labelled "federal," but not others, certainly fewer than in the case of the United States. We already live in a particular kind of European federal state; what we need to do is to determine how that state is to develop. Unless we believe that we should leave the European Union, we must engage fully and realistically in the discussion of the future shape of Europe.

A number of Europeanists are at pains to assert that federalism is not a centralising force. The reality of the centralising effects of federalism depends, however, on the starting point. The devolution of power to the Scottish Parliament and to the Welsh Assembly involves the introduction of federal elements into the British state, but this is a decentralising application of the federal idea. In the case of Europe, of course, it *is* a centralising influence; if you start with six or more sovereign independent states and create an authority over them with binding powers, however minimal, you are inevitably centralising power. The question is to what degree should that centralisation be taken and in what areas; how should it be controlled or limited? The point about federal models of government is that they lie somewhere on a broad spectrum of centralisation, or decentralisation, but the intention of those who advocate a federal model is that federalism represents a technique for trying to control or limit centralisation – as was the model that Madison evolved for the United States of America. The Madisonian model is a model of limited government, and the British approach to Europe would be more coherent, and more productive, if it were to be based upon the kind of model that Madison evolved. I think that Madison would have agreed with the need for a Constitution for Europe, but he would have disapproved of the Draft European Constitution proposed in 2004 for a number of reasons.

A Constitution for Europe should have as one of its major aims the setting of clear limits to the power of the European Government. However, the Draft European Constitution blurred this distinction in a number of ways.

It is true that Section 2 of Article I-11 of Title III provided that "the Union shall act within the limits of the competences conferred upon it... Competences not conferred upon the Union remain with the Member States," wording not dissimilar to that of the Tenth Amendment to the Constitution of the United States.[30] But the Draft Constitution then modified this principle in a number of ways. It introduced the concept of subsidiarity.[31] Although the draft confined the application of the principle of subsidiarity to the "use of competencies" rather than their conferral, this vague, almost certainly non-judicial, provision would better have been excluded altogether, in spite of the fact that the concept was once embraced by Prime Minister John Major. Furthermore, modifications of the basic principle of the limitation of powers were introduced by the so-called "passerelle clauses," by which in eight areas of power the Council or the European Council could, by a unanimous vote, change the method of voting from unanimity to qualified majority voting.[32]

A major aspect of the legal basis of the European legal structure that needs to be reconsidered is the way in which exclusive power is granted to the European Union over the single market. This is, of course, not a new provision; it lies at the very heart of the European view of economic integration. But it has led to the concept of "harmonisation", to the overbearingly bureaucratic character of the European enterprise. This has even been recognised, in part, by the European Commission. In 2005, launching an initiative to simplify the European regulatory regime, José Manuel Barroso, President of the European Commission, said: "Releasing our creativity from the restraints of red-tape is the best way to push forward our ambitious goals for the economy, for the society and the quality of life of our citizens. If we can improve the regulatory environment both at EU and national level, we will take a giant step towards unlocking Europe's hidden potential." Of course, a comprehensive review of the extent of the powers conferred on the Union is also appropriate, but that is too extensive a subject to be discussed here.

By contrast, the grant of power to the Federal Government by the American Constitution to regulate "commerce among the several states", the Interstate Commerce Clause, has worked well. Although there has been a considerable extension of the power of the Federal Government over the past 200 years as the courts have interpreted the meaning of "commerce" and of "among the several states", the working of the political process in the Congress has moderated the potential effects of Federal power over the minutiae of economic life.

The introduction of some further aspects of the federal model into the European Constitution could be seen as limiting the power of the European Parliament, and the Brussels bureaucracy, rather than enhancing them. If the duty of enforcing European edicts was given to the European bureaucrats directly rather than through the civil servants of the member states, it would give to the servants of Europe a much more realistic view of what the impact of European law actually was on the ground, and of the people's reactions to it. Similarly, direct taxation imposed by the European Parliament rather than by raising money through imposts on member states would make the members of the European Parliament much more aware of the views of their constituents on the desirability of legislation involving expenditure. Modern federalists should perhaps adopt the slogan "No Representation without Taxation" to bring their MEPs to heel.

Finally, the Charter of Fundamental Rights as set out in the Draft Constitution of 2004 needs great simplification. It is very long, ambiguous and confused. One example will suffice: Article II-74 (3) of Title II of the Charter provides that: "The freedom to found educational establishments with due respect for democratic principles and the right of parents to ensure the education and teaching of their children in conformity with their religious, philosophical and pedagogical convictions shall be respected, in accordance with the national laws governing the exercise of such freedom and right." What on earth does that mean? The American Bill of Rights of 1791 was aimed at limiting the power of the newly established Federal Government, which it was feared could become oppressive. In fact it was the states, particularly in the South, that became oppressive to minority groups, and similar restraints upon the powers of the states were eventually imposed by the Supreme Court in the twentieth century through the application of the Fourteenth Amendment. The whole tenor of the proposed European Charter of Fundamental Rights is very different, reflecting the very different nature of society and government today. However, the Charter needs to be shortened, and divided up into three parts, setting limits to the exercise of power by the Union over individuals, setting limits to the powers of national governments over individuals, and providing a framework for the rights of the individual against the actions of others.

What we need to do then is to face the challenge of the present point in our history, to determine what we want to do, and then, avoiding "politics by slogan", to have a sensible and frank discussion of a future constitution for

Europe, something that has so far not happened in Britain outside of academic circles.

Of course, the more timid amongst us will refer to the fact that we cannot foresee what the consequences of our actions will be in 200 years' time; maybe Europe will evolve into a state as centralised as the United States is today, but maybe we can prevent an even greater centralisation of power in Europe, which could be the more serious threat, both to those in the Union and to those who stay out.

Notes to Chapter 1

1   Ralph Ketcham, *James Madison: A Biography* (Charlottesville and London: University Press of Virginia, 1990), p. 170. My paper owes a great deal to this brilliant biography of Madison.
2   Ketcham, pp. 145-7.
3   See Kevin Phillips, *The Cousins' Wars: Religion, Politics, and the Triumph of Anglo-America* (New York: Basic Books, 1999).
4   Bruce A. Ackerman, *The Failure of the Founding Fathers: Jefferson, Marshall, and the Rise of Presidential Democracy* (Cambridge, Mass. and London: Harvard University Press, 2005), pp. 14-15.
5   Quoted in Phillips, p.327.
6   Ketcham, p. 137.
7   Ackerman, p.11.
8   M.J.C. Vile, *Constitutionalism and the Separation of Powers,* 2nd edition (Indianapolis: Liberty Fund, 1998).
9   Vile, pp. 53-6.
10 David Hume, 'Of the Original Contract', in *Essays*, George Routledge and Sons (no date).
11 David Hume, *Essays,* p.367. See Ketcham, p. 187.
12 Charles Louis de Secondat, Baron de Montesquieu, *De l'Esprit des Lois* (Paris: 1748), Book XI, Chapter VI.
13 Vile, pp.111-4.
14 Alfred H. Kelly, Winifred A. Harbison and Herman Belz, *The American Constitution: Its Origins and Development,* Volume I, 7th edition (New York, London: Norton, 1991), p. 39.
15 *ibid.*, p. 62.
16 N. Feldman, 'The Voidness of Repugnant Statutes: Another Look at the Meaning of *Marbury*', in *Proceedings of the American Philosophical Society*, Vol. 148, No. 1. March, 2004, p.31.
17 Vile, pp.137-8.
18 Kelly, Harbison and Belz, I, pp. 46-50.
19 Henry Steele Commager, *Documents of American History*, 7th edition (New York: Appleton-Century-Crofts, 1965), pp. 26-28.
20 *ibid.*, pp. 80-81.
21 Ketcham, p. 50.

[22] John Taylor of Caroline, *An Inquiry into the Principles and Policy of the Government of the United States,* 1814, reprinted with an introduction by Roy Franklin Nichols (Routledge and Kegan Paul, 1950).

[23] Alexander Hamilton, James Madison and John Jay, *The Federalist or, The New Constitution*, edited by William R. Brock (London: Phoenix Press, 2000), pp. 83-88.

[24] *The Federalist*, p. 239.

[25] Commager, pp. 182-3.

[26] Ketcham, pp. 396-7.

[27] *Printz v. United States*, 521 U.S. 898 (1997).

[28] Ketcham, p.181.

[29] Michael Burgess, *Comparative Federalism: Theory and Practice* (London: Routledge, 2006), pp. 29 ff.

[30] *The European Constitution in Perspective: Analysis and Review of 'The Treaty Establishing A Constitution for Europe,* British Management Data Foundation, 2004.

[31] The Draft Constitution states: "Under the principle of subsidiarity, in areas which do not fall within its exclusive competence, the Union shall act only if and insofar as the objectives of the proposed action cannot be sufficiently achieved by the Member States, either at central level or at regional and local level, but can rather, by reason of the scale or effects of the proposed action, be better achieved at Union level." Title III, Article I-11, section 3. On the concept of subsidiarity see Andrew Duff (ed.), *Subsidiarity within the European Community* (London: Federal Trust, 1993).

[32] *The European Constitution in Perspective*.

Chapter 2

The British Tradition of Federalism: Nature, Meaning and Significance

Michael Burgess

IT IS A DECADE SINCE THE LABOUR GOVERNMENT OF TONY BLAIR IMPLEMENTED THE CONSTITUTIONAL PROJECT that formally introduced devolution for Scotland and Wales, and produced the bundle of reforms that enabled Northern Ireland to anticipate a new beginning for self-government in that troubled part of the United Kingdom (UK). In short, the all-round package of constitutional reform proposals – part of the Labour government's modernising agenda – brought to a close the long struggle to overhaul the British system of parliamentary government that harked back to the 1880s and 1890s when the motto of the late Victorian constitutional discourse that was dominated by "Home Rule for Ireland" was extended to "Home Rule All Round."[1] It meant Irish, Scottish and Welsh home rule as part of a grand package that would reduce the weight of legislation on an overburdened House of Commons, solve the Irish imbroglio and nip Scottish and Welsh nationalism in the bud. The Irish Question therefore prompted both the leading political thinkers of the day and the practitioners of government to reconsider constitutional reform in the wider context of a wholesale root and branch overhaul of the British Constitution.

Today the prospects for genuine decentralisation in the Union State that is now the UK seem extremely positive.[2] A new political dynamic has been introduced into relations between the constituent parts of the union – intragovernmental relations have been replaced by intergovernmental relations - and there is plenty of evidence to suggest that this represents a marked change in the overall British political culture. But the devolution story to date has not ended the public debate about the democratic nature of this curious polity that is the UK. The optimism about the future of the British polity that characterised support for devolution in the 1990s has been qualified in several ways. The position of England within the Union State remains anomalous in many important respects, the fiscal powers of Scotland, Wales and Northern Ireland that are so crucial to a vibrant decentralised state remain weak. The question of the reform of the House of Lords, the second chamber of the central legislature, remains unresolved.

These conspicuous lacunae in the constitutional project are serious obstacles to the fulfilment of Labour's modernisation goals and they are also impediments to a revitalised British liberal democracy.

The failure to arrive at some kind of broad-based agreement about completing the circle of devolution by extending the current reform to the English polity – usually construed as English Home Rule – has left the impression of a project that is unfinished and incomplete. The British project is lopsided; it has deepened democracy in three of the four constituent parts of the Union State but it has failed to match these developments with similar reforms in England.[3] Moreover, by devolving powers to Scotland, Wales and Northern Ireland without a major overhaul of central institutional relations that would reorder the representational links between the different parts of the British polity, this asymmetrical devolution has left the polity by default to function with some serious design faults. The old unitary state used to work on the basis of a series of flexible understandings based on conventions, customs and usages, and while the new union state still works it does so only on the basis of stretching such understandings to new limits.

This qualified optimism about British devolution derives from a strong sense of unease in the body politic that can be traced back over a century ago to when the movement for Home Rule All Round first became a serious practical project. It was the first time that senior statesmen like Joseph Chamberlain, Lord Rosebery, David Lloyd George and Winston Churchill engaged the subject directly in their private correspondence, public speeches and parliamentary debates. During the first decade of the twentieth century United Kingdom devolution – otherwise known as federalism – was part and parcel of the mainstream constitutional and political discourse of the day and was widely understood to mean the granting of subordinate local national assemblies for England, Scotland, Wales and Ireland.[4] Indeed, it is in this light that we can begin to appreciate how far devolution itself and the continuing debate about the nature of the union state is actually an integral part of the larger British tradition of federalism.

Contemporary concerns about institutional design, electoral reform, different forms of political representation, House of Lords reform and the business of parliamentary legislation were all rehearsed during these years, leaving a rich deposit of written evidence available to us today in the continuing public debate about the constitutional architecture of the British state. This is now a political resource and we are able to draw on this historical evidence in our efforts to obtain that invaluable sense of perspective without which we cannot properly understand and appreciate the nature of the contemporary debate. The terms federalism and devolution have been woven into the fabric of this public debate so much so that it is now impossible to explore the implications of the one without the other. Moreover, the connection between these two terms of the political discourse has been strengthened by contemporary developments in European integration, especially the current negotiation and ratification processes of the Constitutional Treaty of the European Union (EU).

The purpose of this chapter is to call attention to the British tradition of federalism and principally to demonstrate its contemporary links to devolution in the UK and British membership of the EU.[5] It is imperative that the existence of this political tradition is neither overlooked nor forgotten because it continues to inform contemporary debates and discussions about how we organise the British polity as a functioning liberal democracy in the EU. In a general sense the British tradition of federalism can be understood as a perfectly legitimate political response to the perceived challenges to the integrity of the British state that date back at least to the mid-Victorian period of the 1870s, but we can also easily trace British federal ideas to the imperial experience of the New World in colonial America in the eighteenth century. This is why it is important for us to begin our survey with the British imperial experience. Strange as it may initially seem, the British Empire itself was one fertile source of federal ideas. Its constitutional evolution in the nineteenth century lent great credence to federalism as an instrument of imperial reorganisation, colonial nation-building and ultimately federal state-formation. Indeed, the British Colonial Office gradually acquired a famous reputation for its ability to "export" British federal ideas that were successfully translated into practical federal experiences in Canada, Australia, India, Malaysia and Nigeria. Other federal experiments that were also tried but failed to stand the test of time were launched under British auspices in New Zealand, the West Indies, Rhodesia and Nyasaland and Central Africa.

In his *Federalism: Origin, Operation, Significance*, first published in 1964, William Riker noted in this seminal contribution to the theoretical debate about federalism that "over one-third of the federalisms existent today have been constructed by uniting former British colonies." This observation led him to ponder whether "there is something in the British political tradition that is especially conducive to the federal form." His meditations quickly prompted him to confirm that "I am sure there is, although I have never been able to identify what it is in a way that is satisfactory to me."[6] In hindsight, Riker's puzzlement about what he called "the British penchant for federalism" can easily be appreciated, especially at a time when the much-vaunted Westminster Model, renowned for producing strong stable government in the centralised unitary state, seemed to point in the opposite direction to federal forms of government.[7] However, as we shall see in this chapter, Riker was not aware of the existence of a distinct British tradition of federalism that was an integral part of the larger British political tradition and, indeed, one that was not only for export but also for the British themselves.

We will address Riker's quest to identify the nature, meaning and significance of the British federal tradition by structuring the chapter around three policy arenas that can serve as conceptual lenses for our brief historical analysis - Empire, Ireland and Europe. These lenses enable us to establish in turn a clear understanding of British imperial policy, Irish policy and European policy and their complex interrelationship in the years since 1870.

Empire

There exists a basic continuity of British federal ideas in the nineteenth and twentieth centuries in the imperial context and it was expressed not only in plans and schemes for the self-governing colonies but also for the British themselves. It emerged gradually in the latter part of the nineteenth century as the British began to think seriously about the future of the empire. The constitutional and political evolution of the white self-governing empire – Canada, Australia and South Africa in particular – suggested that these colonies were logically destined at some undefined point in the future to acquire fully-fledged independence from the mother country. This was at a time when contemporary events and circumstances seemed to herald a new age of military and commercial competition, especially in Europe with the rise of Germany after Prussia's sweeping victory over France in 1871, Russia's unilateral abrogation of the Black Sea Clauses in 1870 and in North America, too, with the consolidation of the United States of America after the Civil War (1861-5).

The mid-Victorian era witnessed a sudden and dramatic surge in the popularity of the federal idea around 1870. In retrospect, 1870 was an important turning point in the growing appeal and relevance of federalism in British politics. It furnished all the basic ingredients necessary for a serious reappraisal of the challenges that confronted the British state: perceived economic decline; a significant shift in international power relations against British imperial hegemony; the mounting menace of Ireland, symptomatic of a breakdown in elite relations; and the challenge to traditional political certainties posed by urban enfranchisement in 1867. In short, the mid-Victorian years between 1860 and 1880 encapsulated a series of major challenges to the old order amounting to nothing less than what Jim Bulpitt has called the modernisation of territorial politics.[8]

The first significant political response to this combination of implied threats and challenges to the British state was the emergence of the imperial federation movement. Its very appearance – at first tentative and inchoate – in 1871 on the occasion of a public meeting held at the Westminster Palace Hotel in London to discuss colonial questions was a landmark in British imperial history. However, it was not then recognised for what it really was: an essentially defensive reaction and response that reflected the mid-Victorian search for a new political and economic relationship with the white self-governing colonies. The phrase imperial federation, so widely used in the vocabulary of British politics for nearly fifty years after 1870, was really a convenient vehicle and rallying cry for those who sought a much more binding and regulated empire but who could not agree upon the details of how it should be achieved. In practice, it was a mobilising ploy for the imperialism of consolidation rather than expansion. Most of those who sympathised with this vague ideal did not really believe that utilisation of the federal principle meant superimposing on the empire the full paraphernalia of a federal constitution analogous to that of the United States of America. Such activists who worked to that end were in a tiny minority. Most imperial federationists sought an undefined closer union either by adjustments in traditional British trading practices or by changes in imperial defence, especially naval defence, which would leave free trade intact. This still left available a very extensive range of empire federalist schemes and proposals which permitted numerous variations of the federal idea.[9] Ged Martin put it thus: "In fact, between 1820 and 1870 a debate about the federal nature of the Empire can be traced. ... It is, however, fair to think of one single movement for a federal Empire throughout the nineteenth century. There is a clear continuity in ideas, in arguments, and in the people involved."[10]

Throughout the 1870s the federal idea, loosely referred to as imperial federation, was hotly debated both in the Royal Colonial Institute (originally established as the Royal Colonial Society in 1868) and in the plethora of articles and essays appearing in the vibrant mid-Victorian press and review literature.[11]

By 1884 the politics of imperial consolidation had crystallised sufficiently to create and sustain the Imperial Federation League dedicated to "the permanent unity of the empire by some form of federation" which would not interfere with the existing rights of local parliaments in the conduct of local affairs. Between 1884 and 1893, when it was abruptly dissolved, the league represented the most important public expression of the idea of closer imperial union during the late-Victorian years. Under the notable political leadership of William Edward Forster, Lord Thomas Brassey and Lord Rosebery, 31 local branches were formed throughout England and Scotland during this period and elite membership hovered at around the figure of 2,000. Moreover, it succeeded in establishing many branches in the Australian colonies, Canada, New Zealand, Cape Town, Barbados and British Guiana. Even if it received only modest public support, the movement itself had been effective in promoting federation as a subject worthy of serious public debate for nearly a quarter of a century.

In 1892 the league finally translated its vague vision into a practical reality when it produced a concrete scheme for imperial federation, even if in reality it was no more than a federal instalment and it was predicated on imperial defence. The proposal boiled down to a council of the empire composed of members appointed by Britain and the self-governing colonies. Britain, Canada and the Australian and South African colonies would be directly represented; whilst India and the crown colonies would be only indirectly represented by the appropriate secretaries of state in charge of their affairs. The council might include – in addition to the representatives of the three great self-governing groups of colonies – the British Prime Minister, Foreign Secretary, Colonial Secretary, First Lord of the Admiralty, Chancellor of the Exchequer and the Secretaries of State for War and India. Unfortunately the scheme studiously avoided defining the proposed council's functions, presuming that they would evolve slowly in the future according to changing circumstances, although it is clear that they were to deal primarily with foreign policy and imperial defence. Predictably Gladstone rejected the scheme in April 1893. The British Prime Minister regarded it as too vague and deficient to warrant serious practical consideration.[12]

Overall federal union within the empire was generally viewed as something for the remote future. Many sympathisers regarded it as desirable but too visionary during the nineteenth century. But when Gladstone's rejection of the federal plan precipitated the league's collapse in 1893, federal ideas did not disappear with it. On the contrary, their resilience was manifested in the variety of small pressure groups which sprouted in Britain during the 1890s. Apart from the Royal Colonial Institute, which had nurtured such ideas for a generation, the Imperial Federation (Defence) Committee emerged in 1894 as evidence that the cause of imperial unity had been reorganised along more specific lines. It coexisted briefly with the United Empire Trade League (1891) and the British Empire League (1896), but federal ideas about empire soon resurfaced in more robust shape during the first decade of the twentieth century when the Round Table movement was formed in 1909 - 10. Destined to dominate British intellectual thinking about Empire-Commonwealth relations until the early 1920s, the movement served as a crucial repository of imperial federationist ideas which represented a basic continuity of thought and practice between the late nineteenth and the early twentieth centuries in terms of the reorganisation of the British state.

Imperial federation was the link which ran beneath the surface of the activities of public men like Lionel Curtis and Philip Kerr, later Lord Lothian, who were among the founders of the new political movement in Edwardian England.[13] This connection was expressed in the nebulous term organic union but it is clear that "the discovery of some form of federation which shall be at once effective and acceptable" was the main focus for their energies.[14] Their main strategy, like that of the Imperial Federation League, was to popularise the federal idea and to seek to influence official thinking, but there the similarity ended. They avoided the mistakes of their predecessors. Concentrating less on mass support than on influencing political leadership, they recognised that widespread popular support was valuable only after politicians had raised the issue. This, as Ged Martin observed, determined their tactics: "major policy problems, like the role of India in a federal union, were thrashed out in secret memoranda. Lobbying was confined to the powerful."[15] As the historian of the movement, John Kendle, remarked: "the movement, particularly the London group, did have some influence in government circles in Great Britain and in the Dominions, not least because its members came from the affluent, the well-placed, the intellectual, and generally the most acceptable members of society."[16]

Agreement upon the definition of their purpose however did not automatically stretch to unanimity about the ultimate form of union to be pursued. Curtis's mystical faith in the British Empire and his almost doctrinaire commitment to the cause of imperial federation was not shared by Kerr. The latter believed fervently in empire but was less than sanguine about attempts to "fit the empire into the constitutional ideas which have suited the United Kingdom and the self-governing colonies in the past." This, in his view, would be to court destruction. The empire would be lost forever. But Kerr did share Curtis's interest in a major reorganisation of the imperial structure and he concurred about the need for a common policy in defence and foreign affairs. He was fully alive to the strengths and sensitivities of colonial nationalism, however, and this awareness made him cautious about what precise form the new political system should take. He preferred merely to acknowledge the desire for a closer, more binding, imperial union.

With the exception of Curtis, the *Round Table* movement determined not to force the pace unnecessarily. Under Kerr's influence as editor of the journal Round Table, the movement preferred to educate British and colonial public opinion to the need for constitutional reform. As always, Kerr felt more comfortable when specific schemes and blueprints were eschewed. They were, in his view, premature and unhelpful. Only when international circumstances changed and after a long period of discussion between the British and colonial governments were concrete initiatives and proposals liable to be well received. Meanwhile federal ideas would continue to circulate and form part of what he viewed as the crucial preliminary intellectual spadework necessary to alter official attitudes and perceptions regarding constitutional change.

As with the imperial federationists of the late-Victorian years, many Round Table enthusiasts favoured the idea of colonial representatives sitting in the British Parliament while others sought to devise new executive machinery to facilitate more effective co-operation and consultation in defence and foreign policy. In this matter the Round Table was unanimous: if the white self-governing colonies (now called Dominions) were to have an effective voice in imperial policy, the quadrennial colonial conferences of the Edwardian years were palpably inadequate. Lionel Curtis was adamant about this. Curtis, a former town clerk of Johannesburg, dubbed "the Prophet" by his admirers, launched himself with single-minded determination on the path towards a federal reconstruction of the empire. His famous *Green Memorandum*, published and widely circulated in 1910, outlined the movement's aims and assumptions, with a detailed plan of imperial federation acknowledging the separation of domestic and imperial affairs. The new institutional framework would include an Imperial Parliament, distinct from Westminster, with a directly elected lower house and an upper house of states based upon equal representation together with an impartial tribunal to decide disputes over legislative jurisdiction between the federal authority and the constituent governments. These far-reaching reforms entailed the creation of a much more narrowly based domestic government for the UK (since the new federal government would deal only with imperial matters and not with the internal affairs of the UK) and the adjustment of British status, concerning internal affairs, with regard to Canada, Australia, New Zealand and South Africa. Various concessions to national sovereignty were incorporated in Curtis's scheme. He was, for example, scrupulously careful to leave the regulation of tariffs alone and he devised an ingenious method for the raising and collection of revenues for imperial purposes. Curtis's plan, in short, contained virtually all of the institutional checks and balances conventionally associated with a modern federation.[17]

A strong sense of mission propelled Curtis into the Dominions during 1910 with a threefold purpose: to disseminate the movement's ideas; to establish Round Table groups among the elite and professional classes; and to maximise the impact of his own memorandum. He met with variable success. His influence appears to have been greatest in Australia and New Zealand where he was able convincingly to depict "the Imperial Problem" as "the Empire in danger," successfully exploiting Antipodean anxieties about both German and Japanese expansionist designs in that part of the world. After all, in the event of war they would still be dependent upon Britain. Consequently the threat of war certainly focused Dominion attention upon the deficiencies of the existing imperial/colonial conference system of consultation. There was undoubtedly a growing belief in the Dominions that a constitutional void existed which could be successfully filled only by new executive machinery devised to respond smoothly in times of crisis. Curtis's proposals and the force of his argument therefore struck a responsive chord in several informed colonial circles. His timing seemed opportune.

The crisis that the Round Tablers had been waiting for arrived in 1914 with the onset of the First World War. Here, at last, was an opportunity to confront the basic lacuna in the British imperial system. In 1916 Curtis published *The Problem of the Commonwealth* which reiterated the urgent need for a common foreign policy. With Lord Alfred Milner, the Round Table's inspiration and idol, entering Lloyd George's Cabinet in 1916 and both Philip Kerr and Waldorf Astor joining the Prime Minister's "Garden Suburb" in the same year, the prospects for the federal idea at the forthcoming Imperial War Conference to be summoned in 1917 seemed highly promising. No supreme federal organ emerged, however. The conference did produce the Imperial War Cabinet with (briefly) executive powers in which all autonomous governments were represented, but it only just outlasted the war, to represent the empire at the Versailles Peace Conference. With it faded the vision of a common imperial government. It would be difficult to take issue with Ged Martin's conclusion: "1917 marked both the greatest triumph and the final defeat of the imperial federation movement."[18]

The First World War brought the existing debate about imperial federation to a practical conclusion: the reality of dominion nationalism and the contribution of the different parts of the empire to victory in that great convulsion precipitated the metamorphosis of empire into commonwealth. The constitutional and political relations between Britain and her imperial offspring were changed forever and the formal relationship was crystallised in the Statute of Westminster in 1931. In consequence historians have usually dismissed the imperial federation movement of the period from the 1870s to the early 1920s as merely a footnote in the overall evolution of the British Empire. Their conventional view is that it had only a marginal significance in the history of British imperial relations. However, they have been looking at the movement only from a particular perspective. If we adopt a different historical perspective, the political movement assumes a new importance. In this light, William Riker could be forgiven for failing to understand that the "British penchant for federalism" in the specific context of empire can be explained as an integral part of the British tradition of federalism. British federal ideas were not solely for export, but were also demonstrably for the British themselves. Let us turn now to look at the Irish dimension to this tradition that serves to buttress our thesis.

Ireland

In his *Federalism and Constitutional Change*, first published in 1956, William Livingston, a leading American scholar of federalism, reminded us not to ignore the presence of certain federal elements in British society and in the processes of British government. Indeed, he claimed that the "many elements of federalism in the British society, and the diversities that constitute this federal quality," were the direct consequence of tradition that binds so much of practice.[19] An integral feature of these diversities that Livingston recognised as federal elements in the British political tradition was the multinational character of the UK. Richard Rose observed that each territorial part of the UK came under the crown "by a separate act, specific to particular historical circumstances and reflecting local conditions" so that the historical processes of state building and national integration in this country were not part of any deliberate, logical plan or the product of any particular ideology.[20] The complex and subtle processes by which England's constitutional and political authority was gradually extended formally to incorporate Wales (1536), Scotland (1707) and Ireland (1801) in first the mainland of Great Britain and then (with the incorporation of Ireland) the United Kingdom reflect a "multiplicity of historical events" that produced a composite consolidated British state with four distinct nations. The UK, then, was not, as Rose reminds us, a natural entity. No reflection of a single national identity, it could not be as considered "a conventional nation-state."[21] It was a union state: a state created by several cumulative bilateral arrangements.

It is in this particular context that we must construe what became known as the Irish problem, although in reality it was actually a British problem. Ireland's place in the British polity has always been contested by a majority of Irish people and its relations with the mainland have always been both troubled and troublesome. During the late nineteenth and early twentieth centuries the Irish problem dominated British government and politics. But the Anglo-Irish relationship from the Act of Union of 1800 to the Government of Ireland Act of 1920 may also be characterised as a veritable seedbed of constitutional reform ideas and proposals. Dissatisfaction with the union of Ireland with Great Britain proved fertile ground for a wide range of constitutional initiatives which included local government reform, devolution, home rule, federation and the outright repeal of the union, leading to Irish independence. George Boyce even went as far as to claim that "British federalism is an Irish invention." "Without the Irish case," he argued, "it is safe to say that federalism would hardly have merited serious political discussion in the British Isles; or at least would not have moved beyond discussion and into the policy process."[22] He was wise to qualify this statement. Clearly the very structure of the UK – and of Great Britain before it – has always rendered elite discussions of the federal idea in the British polity perfectly intelligible and legitimate. Indeed, Livingston was right: federal or quasi-federal elements have always been immanent in the historical and socio-cultural fabric of British society.

Federalism was advocated in the 1870s by Isaac Butt and his Home Rule party, but it was during the 1880s that federal ideas first began to circulate widely among those politicians and statesmen who sought a practical solution to the Irish problem. The relationship between federalism and Ireland in the UK, however, was never a simple one. It was subjected to numerous cross-currents of opinion. Two examples convey the complexity of this relationship in our brief survey. First, there was the link with the integrity of the British Empire. In late-Victorian England, as already demonstrated, federalism and the Irish question could never be completely divorced from the imperial dimension. The problem of Ireland was always viewed in terms of the integrity of the UK, but during this period any reorganisation of Anglo-Irish constitutional relations would also have to be consistent with the unity of the empire. Indeed, it was inextricably linked to the wider question of imperial unity. Construed in this way an Irish separation – tantamount to an imperial disintegration – was simply unthinkable. Indeed, set in its imperial context many advocates of a reconstructed federal relationship between mainland Britain and the island of Ireland also viewed this as the *sine qua non* of a wider scheme of imperial federation. Consequently a federal solution to the Irish problem would presage the wholesale reconstruction of the empire into a more binding union.

Secondly, since federalism emphasised ideas of local autonomy and self-government within a larger union, the view that it should be extended to include the whole of the UK was certainly logical. Why limit the federal solution to Ireland? The reconstitution of the UK as a federal state would remedy many of its outstanding problems. It would solve the Irish imbroglio; it would resolve the question of legislative congestion and relieve an overburdened Parliament; it would make for more efficient local government; it would correspondingly facilitate more time for the discussion of imperial affairs; and it could conceivably pave the way for some form of imperial federation. Federal ideas tended therefore to become enmeshed in the Irish question in a very complicated manner. Indeed, as we have already noted, discussions about federalism and Ireland led assuredly to "Home Rule all round" and imperial federation.

These two examples of the complexity of the relationship between federalism and the Irish problem confirm that the key to understanding the politics of constitutional reform from the period of the 1880s to the early 1920s lies in the complicated relationship between the UK and its empire. Boyce may have been correct when he observed that "Federalism gave the Irish problem a British dimension, and the British problem an Irish dimension," but it also added another, imperial, dimension.[23] In this context the federal idea was both resilient and ubiquitous precisely because it bridged the three dimensions of mainstream constitutional discourse: the imperial; the (multinational) UK state; and the major constituent sub-state national territories of England, Scotland, Wales and Ireland. Small wonder that this Rubik's Cube of its day should lead political elites to misuse terms and treat home rule, devolution, and home rule all round as if they were synonymous with federalism. "Imperial federation" itself suffered as much from this confusion and misunderstanding as it did to perpetuate it.

Bulpitt construes two specific historical periods – the 1880s and the years between 1910 and 1926 – as amounting to "conditions of territorial crisis" in the UK when the traditional territorial order was seriously threatened by the major challenge of modernisation.[24] John Kendle also claimed that the question of Irish self-government provoked a much larger constitutional discussion about the territorial structure and the distribution of power within the UK.[25] Clearly it is important to emphasise the historical continuity of the British tradition of federalism, but we must also identify within it three separate episodes during these years when the federal idea entered the public policy domain as a practical proposal worthy of serious consideration. These three episodes relate to Joseph Chamberlain, federalism and Ireland (1885-6); United Kingdom devolution (1910-14); and

Ireland and "Home Rule all round" (1917-8). We will consider each of them separately.

a) Joseph Chamberlain, federalism and Ireland, 1885-6

Joseph Chamberlain's role in the Liberal party split of 1886 has been well documented but it remains the subject of constant debate and reappraisal by historians. He played a crucial role in the failure of Gladstone's first home rule bill in the House of Commons in June 1886 and subsequently, along with Lord Hartington, led the dissentient Liberal Unionists into permanent opposition to Gladstone's policy for Ireland. However, while most of the facts about Chamberlain's views on the Irish question have long been well known, the overall significance of his federal ideas has been underestimated. His measured sympathy for imperial federation has been largely ignored and dismissed in the mainstream literature.

In retrospect, the scepticism with which some historians have treated Chamberlain's opinions about federalism and the way that they became entwined in the epic public debate about Ireland during 1885-6 is understandable. His federal ideas appear to have developed in a somewhat haphazard fashion. They were both confused and confusing. This was doubtless because they crystallised under the sudden pressure of the Irish problem in 1885 but much remains unclear. His main political strategy was to defeat the Gladstone bill rather than to promote an alternative scheme. Nonetheless, there was sufficient consistency in Chamberlain's thinking to suggest that federalism was more than mere opportunism. His support for the federal solution can be traced back at least to 1874 when he approved Isaac Butt's proposal, called a "federal arrangement," and an advanced form of devolution was firmly incorporated in the famous Radical Programme of 1885.[26] The primary aim of what would be a drastic reorganisation of British government was the devolution of parliamentary business which would improve the efficiency of legislation by freeing the imperial parliament to confine itself to foreign affairs, trade, defence and Indian and colonial matters in general.

It is certain that by the autumn of 1885 Chamberlain's mind had begun to contemplate the federal idea. His own preference was to situate Ireland in terms of local government reform for the whole of the UK. This meant setting up a series of county boards and national councils so as to distinguish between all local matters pertaining to counties and those larger domestic affairs that necessarily transcended individual counties but could be satisfactorily accommodated within England, Scotland, Wales and Ireland. This reform possessed several merits: it would have given Ireland domestic control of purely domestic affairs; treated each constituent nation equally; relieved the imperial parliament of congestion; and ensured that parliamentary sovereignty remained unimpaired. However, the firm refusal of the Irish national leader, Charles Stewart Parnell, to countenance such a scheme impelled Chamberlain to move swiftly, under the pressure of Gladstone's home rule initiative, and cast around in a despairing effort to consider a wide range of constitutional possibilities. Kendle makes it clear that by the end of 1885 Chamberlain was "familiar with federal systems" and that his determination not to offer Ireland anything more than he would concede to either England or Scotland drove him to address the federal idea as a possible solution.[27] There is no other way of explaining Chamberlain's sudden willingness during 1885-6 to give serious thought to some form of federation for the UK as a whole.

Kendle claimed "it is not fully clear what Chamberlain meant by federalism, although it would seem that, for a time at least, he did seriously consider a true division of sovereignty." This view contrasts sharply with that of Richard Jay who believed that there were "grounds for doubting his seriousness in advocating it."[28] What is indisputable is that federalism emerged as one of the most significant features of the momentous debate on Irish home rule in the House of Commons in 1886 and Chamberlain played a key role in this shifting emphasis. When he made his memorable parliamentary announcement on 9 April 1886 that the solution to the Irish problem might be found in some form of federation he kindled a fire that spread rapidly throughout the House. In hindsight it seems clear that Chamberlain did wrestle with federation as a potential solution to the Irish question but only briefly and under extenuating circumstances. Jay's assertion that "almost alone, Chamberlain in the 1880s grappled with the idea of separate assemblies for Dublin and Belfast" is a useful reminder of the Birmingham radical's imaginative boldness.[29] It is also an indicator of the important legacy he left for succeeding politicians who were to tackle the Irish question a quarter of a century later. Chamberlain was the first British politician actively to explore the possibilities of an Irish solution that entailed UK devolution. In widening the scope of the public debate to include England, Scotland and Wales, while broadening the context to encompass imperial implications, his political activities in the 1880s gave impetus and legitimacy to the wider debate about federation in the UK during the next 40 years.

b) United Kingdom devolution, 1910-14

In 1886 and 1893 parliament rejected Irish home rule bills proposed by

Gladstone and the Liberal Party, and the issue was subsequently shelved during the years between 1895 and 1911 largely because of opposition of the House of Lords which exercised a permanent veto over Liberal Government legislation. With passage of the Parliament Act in 1911, however, the way was open for progress to be made on the Irish question because one of the Act's stipulations allowed bills passed by the House of Commons in three successive sessions automatically to receive the Royal Assent. With the main obstacle removed, both major political parties were compelled to adapt and adjust to different constitutional and political circumstances.

During the period surveyed here the Irish problem prompted a continuous stream of constitutional reform ideas and proposals spanning both sides of the traditional British party political divide. These innovative ideas and proposals were not confined to the outer reaches of the British parliament. On the contrary, they penetrated to the very heart of executive cabinet government, reaching the inner sanctum of the British Prime Minister's office and drawing into their embrace both David Lloyd George and Winston Churchill who were compelled to respond to the British federal tradition.

From about the year 1910 it is important to make a distinction between two separate sets of political events and circumstances. First, we must return to acknowledge the highly influential federalist pressure group known as the Round Table movement, which emerged in British politics and played a significant role in the reappearance and reshaping of federal ideas both in terms of the Irish problem and imperial federation. Secondly, the idea of home rule all round finally entered the domain of practical politics. The activities of the Round Table movement have been well documented by Kendle.[30] Both in its origins and its inspiration it was very much an organisation with partisan Unionist sympathies. As we have already seen, it was inspired by Philip Kerr and Lionel Curtis and construed the Irish problem as an imperial question. From about 1910 it attracted other former members of Lord Alfred Milner's "*Kindergarten*" as well as a number of well connected outsiders that included Frederick Scott Oliver, Lord Robert Cecil, Edward Grigg, Waldorf Astor and Leopold Amery. Other notable Unionists who were strong supporters of a federal settlement for the UK were Lord Selbourne, Thomas Allnutt Brassey and Moreton Frewen. Oliver was a highly influential figure in Unionist circles, a well-respected confidant of leading figures in the party and a prolific writer of pamphlets, books, periodical articles and letters to newspapers who in 1906 had written an outstanding treatise on federalism in the form of a biography of Alexander Hamilton. His ubiquitous influence upon British policy makers was, as we shall see, to reach its apogee in 1918 owing to the urgency of the Irish question, but it is Kerr and Curtis who are of special and enduring significance to the British federal tradition because together they made an enormous contribution to the overall evolution of British political ideas that straddled a generation. Their own federal ideas emerged from genuine attempts to resolve British imperial problems, the Irish conundrum and, later, European relations. Empire, Ireland and Europe were the catalysts for change, but change which produced a basic continuity of federal ideas.

Across the party political divide the notion of "home rule all round" during 1910-14 also attracted considerable support in Liberal Party circles, something that, according to Patricia Jalland, has tended to be overlooked: "The Unionist advocates of federalism have received far more attention than the Liberals... yet Home Rule all round won far more sympathy from the Liberal than from Unionist leaders, and gained strong support from the Liberal backbenches, especially among the Scottish Nationalists."[31]

According to Jalland, there were two distinct groups of Scottish Liberals advocating home rule all round for different reasons. The first group could be described as Scottish home rulers who were independently aggressive and eager to use the renewed Liberal interest in Irish home rule as a lever for pressing Scottish demands. Many Scottish Liberals resented the priority given to Irish home rule and saw a larger federal scheme as a means of promoting Scotland's prospects more rapidly. Certainly their overriding preoccupation was with Scottish home rule rather than with either Ireland or a constitutional settlement for the UK. The second and smaller group of Scottish Liberals, however, championed home rule all round on its own merits.

This political background is important when we briefly consider the great success which Lionel Curtis scored on his own terms in 1912. He persuaded the young, rumbustious Winston Churchill to consider and adopt the federal ideas circulating within the Round Table. Churchill, however, was already sympathetic to these ideas, having just presented, along with Lloyd George, the only federal proposals offered to the official cabinet committee on home rule when it commenced its deliberations in February 1911. His position on Irish home rule and home rule all round was much more radical than any of his contemporaries anticipated. He circulated two memoranda in February and March 1911 proposing a full-blown scheme of home rule all round which spelled out a UK divided into ten segments, each with its own assembly for legislative and administrative purposes. A year later it had become obvious that the main obstacle in the path of a third home rule bill for Ireland was the Ulster question – the objection of Ulster Protestants to home rule for the whole of Ireland. Both Churchill and Lloyd George sought a compromise position whereby separate provision could be made for the predominantly Protestant Ulster counties, but to no avail. This was the awkward predicament that persuaded Churchill, in Jalland's words, to "drop his bombshell... for which his colleagues were totally unprepared."[32] In a major speech in Dundee in September 1912 he resurrected his previous federal scheme of 1911 and urged his audience to consider a federal United Kingdom - a reconstructed Albion that included national parliaments for Ireland, Wales and Scotland and regional legislatures for England, all subordinate to an imperial parliament. As First Lord of the Admiralty and a member of the cabinet committee on home rule, whose own federal proposals had already been privately rejected by that same committee, Churchill's decision to go public in Dundee certainly stretched the ministerial line and caused more than a stir with its obvious implications for a separate parliament for Ulster that clearly went against official government policy.

Churchill's undoubted federalist tendencies in the context of Ireland and home rule all round together with his evident disregard for the convention of collective cabinet responsibility guaranteed that "he helped in making federalism a major talking point once more in party and intellectual circles; and it remained at the forefront of the political stage until the early summer of 1914."[33] Despite such pressures and influences, Prime Minister Asquith opted for a modified version of Gladstone's 1893 approach. His caution was a missed opportunity to incorporate into the third Irish home rule bill aspects of federalism deemed synonymous with home rule all round.

c) Ireland and Home Rule all round, 1917-8
In September 1914 this bill became the Government of Ireland Act. However, a Suspensory Act, passed simultaneously, guaranteed that Irish home rule would not be implemented until after the First World War. As Jalland remarked, the outbreak of the war enabled Asquith to escape the consequences of his Irish policy and there was "no evidence to suggest that a political solution would otherwise have been reached, given a little more time."[34] In practice the Irish question was relegated to secondary importance for most politicians in 1914 and did not reoccupy official minds until Lloyd George decided to summon an Irish Convention which met in July 1917 in Dublin under the chairmanship of Sir Horace Plunkett and remained in session until May 1918.

The Irish problem became once again the catalyst for federal ideas and proposals that reached into the very heart of official government circles during the period April to July 1918. The tense climate of the First World War, the Easter Rebellion in 1916 in Dublin, the resignation of Asquith and the arrival of Lloyd George as British Prime Minister in June the same year together with the mounting pressure for conscription in Ireland in 1918 combined to produce a set of circumstances conducive to growing support for varieties of devolution, home rule all round and federalism. Indeed, the dramatic events of March 1918, when the massive German offensive broke through Allied lines and threatened the Channel ports and Paris, acted as a decisive spur that propelled Lloyd George with obstinate determination down the path of military conscription for Ireland combined with a new Irish home rule bill. This dual policy, fiercely opposed in Ireland by both Nationalists (along with the Roman Catholic Church) and the Ulster Unionists, potentially opened a window of opportunity for alternative proposals and schemes for constitutional reform.

It is against this turbulent background that F. S. Oliver's pivotal role in the Irish imbroglio must be understood. Oliver was a close friend of Sir Edward Carson (the leader of the Ulster Unionists), Austen Chamberlain, Lord Selbourne and Lord Alfred Milner and was intimately connected with the network of elite society that was active in Round Table circles. He was a confirmed federalist and had been a consistent champion of home rule all round that would have created a federal UK during the constitutional crisis of 1910 but led instead to the Parliament Act of 1911 and he was active again in that cause during 1913-4. With the assistance of Selbourne, Oliver drafted a pamphlet in June 1917 for private circulation entitled *A Method of Constitutional Cooperation: Suggestions for the Better Government of the United Kingdom* in which they recommended "the solution of the Irish problem by the adoption of a federal government for the United Kingdom."[35] Kendle pointed out that their proposals were prompted by the urgency of the Irish question but this was not their primary concern. Their main object was the better government of the United Kingdom as a whole and the Irish problem was only a part, though an urgent part, of a much larger problem that only federalism could solve. During the months between September 1917 and February 1918 Oliver had instigated a subtle and effective campaign behind the scenes that reached into the heart of British government circles.

With the Irish Convention evidently having great difficulty reaching agreement, Oliver drafted a pamphlet in February 1918 on *Ulster and a Federal Settlement* in which he publicly stated the case for federalism. During this period he used his connections to persuade both Carson and Chamberlain of the urgent need to broach the federal scheme to both Lloyd George and Sir Horace Plunkett in an attempt to influence the government's policy agenda. Using the successful political strategy of the "Selbourne Memorandum" that had been so effective in helping to construct a new constitution for South

Africa in 1909-10, Oliver and Selbourne managed to infiltrate the inner sanctum of the Prime Minister's office via Carson who outlined to the Prime Minister what he described as the only possible solution – a system of federation for the whole United Kingdom. As Boyce and Stubbs observed, "not for the first time, a leading British politician found himself arguing in the sentences and ideas of F. S. Oliver." For a brief moment when Lloyd George appealed for concessions from the Ulster Unionists to allow him to introduce "a reorganisation of the affairs of the United Kingdom on a federal basis" real practical progress seemed possible. It was precisely at this critical juncture, however, that events in the war, noted above, deflected the Prime Minister from this course and diverted his priorities to conscription in Ireland, thus abruptly closing another window of opportunity.[36]

Kendle claims that federalism was "formally dead in British government circles by the end of July" but "in practice it had been since late March 1918." It was killed by the extension of conscription to Ireland.[37] Yet the federal idea had important supporters in Lloyd George's War Cabinet. Its main advocates were Austen Chamberlain and Walter Long and it had a significant sympathiser in General Jan Christian Smuts who agreed "heart and soul... to get the Irish bill on to federal lines."[38] Moreover, the Irish Committee that had been established by the War Cabinet in April 1918 principally to prepare a new home rule bill to be introduced in the House of Commons before the military service bill had passed its third reading was chaired by Long, the Colonial Secretary, and included Chamberlain and Smuts so that "it was apparent that the committee would be working constantly within an ideological framework of federalism." Indeed, "all its thinking on political and financial issues during the next three months (April-June) was determined to some degree by the federal idea."[39] Long informed Lloyd George about the committee's unexpectedly rapid progress and assured him that opinion among the members had hardened in the direction of a federal system largely because once the federal system was adopted the drafting of the bill became easier.

Under the editorship of Geoffrey Dawson, the considerable weight of *The Times* was added to the general campaign in favour of federalism in 1918, releasing its correspondence columns, editorial page and its lead articles to the advocates of federalism while four Scottish MPs and a Unionist, Arnold Ward, put down separate motions in the House of Commons calling for the introduction at the earliest possible moment of a measure of federal home rule applicable to each unit of the UK. Leo Amery also engaged the public debate directly in April 1918 when he prepared the outline of a draft bill along the lines of the earlier Oliver-Selbourne scheme, which presupposed national parliaments for England, Scotland, Wales and Ireland with an overarching UK parliament, and forwarded it to Chamberlain to ensure that it would become part of the Irish Committee's deliberations. This was typical of the overall Round Table political strategy of "permeation" whereby the federalist movement successfully infiltrated the highest echelons of British government in their quest to persuade the political and bureaucratic elites of the merits of the case for a federal UK.

Evidence of the widespread support and sympathy for federal ideas in Parliament at this time can be gauged by reference to Oliver's own estimation that about 50 Unionists, 90 Liberals and an uncertain number of Labour MPs wanted "federation for its own sake." This assessment of support for the federal idea in March 1918 may actually have seriously underestimated the real figure. A personal survey conducted for Lloyd George in May 1918 to weigh the strength of the federalists put their numbers at around 340 MPs stretching across virtually the entire party political spectrum. We can see therefore that 1918 represented yet another crossroads in the overall evolution of the British tradition of federalism. It was the year when federalism reached its apogee in terms of elite opinion and the public policy agenda. Both Lloyd George and Austen Chamberlain agreed that a revised scheme of Irish home rule would have to "fit in with a federal plan" – it would have to be consistent with home rule all round.

In conclusion, 1917-8 was the time when public interest in federalism ran high throughout the UK. The British government came under considerable pressure from both executive and parliamentary elites in favour of the federal solution and it was compelled to consider a practical federal arrangement for Ireland. Unfortunately for the federalists, however, they did not succeed. They were certainly successful in persuading Lloyd George of the merits of federal ideas for Ireland in the context of the UK, but ultimately they could not convince him to adopt one of their many proposals. The outcome of the long protracted elite negotiations and party political manoeuvres in pursuit of a constitutional settlement of the Irish question was the Government of Ireland Act, 1920. This was in many ways a disappointing result because it effectively paved the way for the partition of the island of Ireland. It was also the first territorial rupture in the UK state.

Europe

We have seen how far British federal ideas were propounded because of both the Irish problem and the question of the future of the British Empire, but the third of our three conceptual lenses through which we can trace the evolution of this distinct federal tradition is directly related to British foreign policy and international relations but particularly concern for relations with Europe. Since this aspect of the British tradition of federalism is a major theme in the chapter by Lucio Levi, this section will be relatively brief.

The intellectual and philosophical basis of federal ideas can be identified in the contribution of Sir John Robert Seeley, Regius Professor of Modern History at Cambridge between 1869 and 1895 and chairman of the Cambridge branch of the Imperial Federation League during 1886-93. It begins with Seeley's remarkable speech to the Peace Society on the "United States of Europe" in 1871: "The nations of Europe must constitute themselves into some form of federation... we shall never abolish war in Europe unless we... take up a completely new citizenship. We must cease to be mere Englishmen, Frenchmen, Germans and must begin to take as much pride in calling ourselves Europeans.... Schemes will fail which propose to unite Europe merely by adding together the states that compose it. The individual and not merely the state must enter into a distinct relation to the federation... the federation wanted is a real union of peoples."[40]

Given these prescient reflections about what was needed to remove the causes of war in Europe, Seeley conveyed an idea and urged a political strategy: it would grow slowly but surely in the minds of many public men and women in the following century.[41] It was no accident that his work – an uneasy combination of inductive political science and earnest patriotic commitment – reflected the contemporary trends of his day. Seeley focused on large imperial themes and on the implications of what he saw as the dawn of a new era of big states which German and Italian unification, together with the reassertion of Russian power, seemed to presage in Europe. Like many of his generation he sought salvation in the British Empire, but his own understanding of the relationship between history and politics compelled him in *The Expansion of England*, first published in 1883, to see in the federal idea the consolidation of the British state.[42]

Federation, then, would be the only way to guarantee peace and liberty in an age of large-scale political units. Seeley had fastened on to an important theme in his conception of international relations. The emphasis of his work lay not just in the evolution of political forms; he was also specifically interested in the historical role of what he called "the English state." It was the nation-state "whose emergence to self-realisation in foreign policy in the seventeenth and eighteenth centuries" he traced and whose future "he tried anxiously to make out in the crystal-ball of inductive political science."[43] Seeley's conception of history gave precedence to the present over the past. Understanding the past was important for the present: it could teach policy-makers how to avoid repeating the mistakes of their forebears. The federal idea emerged from this particular juxtaposition of history and politics. Seeley fits into the British tradition of federalism in an obvious way but at two discrete levels: first, his practical political concern for the future of the UK at the dawn of a new era of large states (he viewed Russia and the United States with particular anxiety); and secondly his more general academic interest in the historical evolution of the international states system. The answer to the former consideration was imperial federation while the solution to the latter problem, if his speech to the Peace Society meant anything, was a genuine federation of European states and citizens. It would be a new peace order. The distinguishing hallmark of an international federal union of states and citizens was crucial. As we will see in the chapter by Lucio Levi, it was to feature prominently in the intellectual debate about a federal Europe throughout the next century.

The European dimension to the British federal tradition must be construed as another major challenge and potential solution to the outstanding problems of the UK in the twentieth century. This theme has not always been evident in the mainstream literature on British foreign policy and relations with European powers. Indeed, it has been construed as only a minor strand in conventional British perspectives on European history - that is Continental Europe. However, if we focus our attentions on public men like Lionel Curtis and Philip Kerr (later Lord Lothian) and on the Round Table movement and the Federal Union (formed in 1938), we can clearly detect a continuity of underlying themes that span a century of British political thought about relations with Europe.[44] In retrospect, Seeley's speech to the Peace Society in 1871 should be understood in these terms. His macrocosmic conception of history and international relations revealed the primary cause of war to be inherent in the nation-state itself. This fundamental assumption compelled him to situate the UK in the larger context of a European federation. He did not believe this could be translated into practical politics in the 1870s, but it was nonetheless the logical outcome of his own beliefs about history and politics.

It took the impact of two world wars within a generation before British federal ideas for Europe finally gained the status of a serious practical alternative to the sovereignty of the nation-state as the only way to organise human relations. The idea of a federal Europe was promoted and sustained in a direct intellectual line of thought from Seeley in the Imperial Federation League to Curtis in the Round Table movement and Lothian in the Federal Union. This has produced a British tradition of federalism that has come down to us today via Empire, Ireland and Europe - and these British federal ideas are not just for export. They are actually British federal ideas for the

British. The political movement in support of European integration since the end of the Second World War is one in which British federal ideas have been prominent. They were the intellectual and practical inspiration for Altiero Spinelli whose contribution to the building of a federal Europe is a core theme of the next chapter in this book.

Conclusion: nature, meaning and significance

This chapter has confirmed the existence of a distinct British tradition of federalism. It has demonstrated that British politics in the period from the mid-Victorian era from about the year 1870 up until the present day can be characterised as a reaction and response to major challenges to the territorial state. These challenges – often construed as territorial crises – were deemed sufficiently serious to warrant several bouts of intellectual reassessment and reappraisal of the nature of the British state and society. Empire, Ireland and Europe are the vehicles or conceptual lenses through which, for well over a century, we can identify and track the gradual emergence of federal ideas as a perfectly logical, legitimate response to the outstanding problems of the United Kingdom.

The nature of the British tradition of federalism is essentially one related to adaptation and adjustment to contemporary change both from within and without. It is a tradition that contains a strong body of intellectual and practical political thinking about the structure of the state and the pronounced diversity of society. The historical processes of state building and national integration have bequeathed a territorial configuration and multinational character to the state and society that has always predisposed the UK to federal and federal-type constitutional, legal and political prescriptions. These have been the result of practical responses to practical problems. They reflect that well-known British penchant for political pragmatism and experience rather than theory, and they are rooted in a British political culture that prefers evolution to revolution, that desires change while preserving continuity.

In essence the meaning of the British tradition of federalism should be explained and understood as part of the larger British political tradition. It means an endorsement of liberal democracy, but an authentic liberal democracy that embodies the politics of difference and diversity. This predisposes it to recognise the importance of political participation at different levels or tiers of authority in a body politic in which individuals, groups and communities of varying and overlapping multinational and multicultural persuasions can live side by side in peace and harmony, their conflicts being legitimately played out in multiple federal political arenas.

The logical corollary of this federal predisposition is to promote institutional reforms that can connect the socio-cultural reality of British society with the state. It is to create new political arenas and policy spaces to empower new diversities with self-determination within the state. In this sense devolution in the UK is merely one step forward in the direction of a genuinely participatory democratic federal polity.

The contemporary significance of the British tradition of federalism lies in its infinite scope for the achievement of justice in the domestic polity and in the international arena. It is difficult to imagine anything more important in the world of the twenty-first century. This tradition has always been at its core a moral imperative in British politics but it has now moved beyond mere reaction and response to perceived challenges to the British state to a much grander vision of how to organise human relations. It is in this continuing intellectual vitality and imaginative boldness wedded to enduring visions of the future that eagerly anticipate and embrace change that we must find continuing significance. British federal ideas will remain significant because they possess a basic flexibility grounded in their inherent capacity to accommodate, conciliate and compromise in an age where political empathy based on consent is often sadly lacking.

Notes to Chapter 2

1 See J. Kendle, *Ireland and the Federal Solution: The Debate over the United Kingdom Constitution, 1870-1921* (Kingston and Montreal: McGill-Queen's University Press, 1989).
2 For details about the contemporary circumstances surrounding the debate on devolution in the UK, see the Special Issue of *Publius: The Journal of Federalism*, Vol. 36(1), (Winter 2006).
3 On the conundrum of England in UK devolution, see R. Hazell (ed.), *The English Question* (Manchester: Manchester University Press, 2005).
4 See P. Jalland, 'United Kingdom devolution 1910-14: political panacea or tactical diversion?', *English Historical Review*, Vol. 94, No. 373, (October 1979), pp. 757-85.
5 For the basic conceptual structure of this survey I have drawn upon my earlier work in M. Burgess, *The British Tradition of Federalism* (London: Leicester University Press, 1995).
6 W.H. Riker, *Federalism: Origin, Operation, Significance* (Boston & Toronto: Little, Brown and Company, 1964).
7 Riker, *ibid.*
8 For the argument about historical challenges to the British state and their impact upon centre-periphery elites in the evolving British polity, see J. Bulpitt, *Territory and Power in the United Kingdom* (Manchester: Manchester University Press, 1983).
9 For further details about the early period of the imperial federation movement, see Burgess, *The British Tradition of Federalism*, ch. 2.
10 G. Martin, 'Empire Federalism and Imperial Parliamentary Union, 1820-1870', *Historical Journal*, XVI (1973), pp. 65-92. See also his 'The Idea of Imperial Federation' in R. Hyam and G. Martin, *Reappraisals in British Imperial History* (London: Macmillan, 1975), ch. 6.
11 See T. Reese, *The History of the Royal Commonwealth Society, 1868-1968* (London: Oxford University Press, 1968).
12 The whole episode is detailed in 'The Federal Plan of the Imperial Federation League, 1892', in Burgess, *The British Tradition of Federalism*, pp. 60-70.
13 For further details about Kerr and Curtis respectively, see J. Pinder, 'Prophet not without Honour: Lothian and The Federal Idea', *Round Table*, Vol. 286 (1983), pp. 207-20; A. Bosco, 'Lothian, Curtis, Kimber and the

Federal Union Movement, 1938-1940', *Journal of Contemporary History*, Vol.23 (3), (July 1988), pp. 465-502; J. Turner (ed.), *The Larger Idea: Lord Lothian and the Problem of National Sovereignty* (London: The Historians' Press, 1988) and D. Lavin, *From Empire to International Commonwealth: A Biography of Lionel Curtis* (Oxford: Clarendon Press, 1995).

14 J.E. Kendle, *The Round Table Movement and Imperial Union* (Toronto: University of Toronto Press, 1975), p. 64.

15 Martin, 'The Idea of Imperial Federation', p. 133.

16 Kendle, *The Round Table Movement*, p. 305.

17 For the contents of the *Green Memorandum*, see Kendle, *The Round Table Movement*, pp. 74-80. See also Lavin, *From Empire to International Commonwealth*, pp. 111-20.

18 Martin, 'The Idea of Imperial Federation', p. 134.

19 W. S. Livingston, *Federalism and Constitutional Change* (Oxford: Clarendon Press, 1956), pp. 269-72.

20 R. Rose, *Understanding the United Kingdom* (London: Longman, 1982), p. 42.

21 Rose, *ibid.*, p. 5.

22 G. Boyce, 'Federalism and the Irish Question', in A. Bosco (ed.), *The Federal Idea: The History of Federalism from the Enlightenment to 1945* (London: Lothian Foundation Press, 1991), Vol. I, ch. IX, p. 119.

23 Boyce, *ibid.*, p. 121.

24 Bulpitt, *Territory and Power in the United Kingdom*, p. 124.

25 This is one of his basic arguments. See Kendle, *Ireland and the Federal Solution*.

26 See D.A. Hamer (ed.), *The Radical Programme: Joseph Chamberlain and others* (Brighton: Harvester Press, 1971) and D. Thornley, *Isaac Butt and Home Rule* (London: Magibbon and Kee, 1964).

27 Kendle, *Ireland and the Federal Solution*, p. 29.

28 R. Jay, *Joseph Chamberlain: A Political Study* (Oxford: Clarendon Press, 1981), p. 125.

29 Jay, *ibid.*, pp. 327-28.

30 See J. E. Kendle, 'The Round Table Movement and "Home Rule all Round"', *The Historical Journal*, Vol. XI (2), (1968), pp. 332-53, and *The Round Table Movement and Imperial Union*.

31 Jalland, 'United Kingdom devolution', pp. 760-62.

32 Jalland, 'United Kingdom devolution', p. 773. For the influence that the Round Table members had on Churchill after April 1912, see Kendle, 'The Round Table Movement and "Home Rule all Round"', p. 348.

33 For the details of Churchill's role in this whole episode, see Jalland, *ibid.*, pp. 765-66 and 773-75.

34 P. Jalland, *The Liberals and Ireland: The Ulster Question in British Politics to*

1914 (Brighton: Harvester Press, 1980), p. 260.

35 For Selbourne and Oliver's lobbying in the spring of 1918, see Kendle, 'Federalism and the Irish problem in 1918', *History*, Vol. 56 (1971), pp. 210 and 212-14.

36 For the details, see D.G. Boyce and J.O. Stubbs, 'F.S. Oliver, Lord Selbourne and Federalism', *Journal of Imperial and Commonwealth History*, Vol. 5 (1976), pp. 53-81.

37 Kendle, 'Federalism and the Irish problem in 1918', p. 229.

38 See Selbourne's correspondence in April 1918 in Boyce and Stubbs, 'F.S. Oliver, Lord Selbourne and Federalism', p. 72.

39 For this and much of what follows see Kendle, 'Federalism and the Irish problem in 1918'.

40 J.R. Seeley, 'The United States of Europe', *MacMillan's Magazine*, Vol. XXIII (1871), pp. 441-4.

41 For Seeley's political ideas, see D. Wormell, *Sir John Seeley and the Uses of History* (Cambridge: Cambridge University Press, 1980), ch. 6.

42 On Seeley's conception of history and political science, see his *Introduction to Political Science* (London: Macmillan and Co., 1896), and S. Collini et al., *That Noble Science of Politics: A Study in Nineteenth Century Intellectual History* (Cambridge: Cambridge University Press, 1983).

43 Collini et al., *ibid.*, pp. 233-4.

44 On the interwar period in general and Federal Union in particular, see Burgess, *The British Tradition of Federalism*, ch. 6, pp. 133-50.

Chapter 3

Altiero Spinelli and European Federalism: The British Influence

Lucio Levi

ALTIERO SPINELLI BECAME A FEDERALIST DURING WORLD WAR TWO whilst in confinement at Ventotene, a small island in the Tyrrhenian Sea off the coast between Rome and Naples. When he was arrested and then convicted by the fascist special tribunal in 1927, he was just 20 years old and was a leader of the young communists. His solitary reflections in jail led him to choose the value of freedom and to give up communism in 1937. The choice of democracy represented for Spinelli only the beginning of a difficult intellectual journey. What distinguishes his intellectual itinerary from that of other antifascists who gave up communism and chose democracy – be it liberal be it socialist – is the fact that the performance of democracy, such as it was in Britain and France in the inter-war period, was deeply disappointing to him. His judgement on it was severe. Failing to provide effective opposition to the fascist states, it appeared to him as a "great decomposing body." By 1941, however, Britain, alone resisting Nazi power, had transformed itself "in the eyes of all European democrats" into their "ideal homeland."[1]

Einaudi and Robbins: the sources of Spinelli's federalist culture

The encounter in 1939 at Ventotene with Ernesto Rossi, one of the leaders of the liberal-socialist movement "*Giustizia e Libertà*,"[2] whose affinities were "all with the eighteenth century enlightenment, particularly English and French," marked Spinelli for life. Rossi was the vehicle of federalist culture. Spinelli describes his ideological mutation in these terms: "In that place I was born a second time... There my true life began."[3]

In a vivid autobiographical page of his memoirs Spinelli described how he discovered federalism and what are the sources of his federalist thinking: "In a volume of writings by Luigi Einaudi reproducing a few articles he published in the 'Corriere della sera' at the beginning of 1919, using the pen name Junius,[4] ... the author brought the project of the League of Nations before the tribunal of reason, found it wholly groundless, and, recalling the constitutional events which led to the foundation of the United States of America, proposed a real federation uniting under the rule of law the peoples which were getting out of the blood bath.

"In the following years I have often been thinking that really *habent sua fata libelli* (little books have their own destiny). When those pages were written, they were received with indifference and the author himself put them aside, since he did not feel it necessary to dig more deeply into that matter. About twenty years later that book accidentally fell under the eyes of two people who had been living for more than ten years isolated from the rest of the world and were then observing with anxious interest the tragedy that had begun in Europe. We perceived that these pages were not written in vain, since they were beginning to fructify in our minds. Requested by Rossi, who as a professor of economics was authorised to write to him, Einaudi sent him two or three booklets of English federalist literature which had flourished toward the end of the thirties as a result of Lord Lothian's influence. Apart from Lionel Robbins's book *The Economic Causes of War*, which I subsequently translated and which was published by the publishing house Einaudi, I cannot recall the titles or authors of others. But their analysis of the political and economic perversion that nationalism leads to, and their reasoned presentation of the federal alternative, have remained to this day impressed on my memory like a revelation.

Since I was looking for mental clarity and precision, I was not attracted by the foggy and contorted ideological federalism of Proudhon or Mazzini, but by the clean, precise thinking of these English federalists, in whose writings I found a very good method for analysing the chaotic state of affairs into which Europe was plunging and for drawing up alternative prospects."[5]

The list of books, discovered in Spinelli's archives, which he read from 1937 up to 1943, when he was released, enables us to recover what time had erased from his memory.[6] In addition to the above mentioned titles of Einaudi and Robbins, there are three more of Robbins's books, *An Essay on the Nature and Significance of Economic Science, The Great Depression* and *Economic Planning and International Order*, together with a collection of essays by Friedrich Hayek, entitled *Collectivist Economic Planning,* and Samuel Morison's *The Oxford History of the United States*. Apart from two books by Carlo Cattaneo, a nineteenth century Italian federalist who advocated both a United States of

Italy and a United States of Europe, no other federalist work is included in the list.

An anthology of writings of William Beveridge, Lionel Robbins and Altiero Spinelli, including excerpts of the *Ventotene Manifesto*, edited by John Pinder, offers a full elaboration of the argument. In the introduction Pinder writes: "Altiero Spinelli, the greatest prophet and advocate of post-war European federalism, owed more to the British federalist writings than to any other source."[7]

The influence of American constitutionalism

Even *The Federalist Papers* were not among the books of Spinelli's library at Ventotene. This means that what can be considered the Old Testament in the federalist tradition is not among the sources of the *Ventotene Manifesto*.[8] Nonetheless *The Federalist Papers* exerted an indirect influence on Spinelli's thinking, not only through the writings of Einaudi, but also those of Robbins. The latter, summarising the subject of *Economic Planning and International Order* – a book quoted several times in the essays written by Spinelli at *Ventotene after the Manifesto* – affirmed that it "included an analysis of the case for international federation based... on the argument of Hamilton and his fellow authors of *The Federalist*, but applied to the international anarchy of the twentieth century."[9] Moreover, *The Economic Causes of War*, the other Robbins book which Spinelli quoted in his Ventotene essays – a book which both Spinelli and Rossi [10] claim to have translated into Italian, a controversy which historians have not yet solved – was an attempt to apply to the contemporary world the theory of the authors of *The Federalist*, which shows that the ultimate cause of war lies in state sovereignty, not in capitalism.

All this shows that both the British and the Italian federalists have common ancestors: the Founding Fathers of the Constitution of the United States of America, and a common cultural matrix, American constitutionalism. The transition of the United States from confederation to federation shows that with a federal government a system of independent states can achieve an irreversible unity and a durable peace. The American Civil War is the exception which proves the rule. In other words, constitutional federalism represents the remedy to international anarchy and a powerful instrument to overcome international economic disorder.

The crisis of the nation-state

Beside American constitutionalism, there is a second theoretical pillar in Spinelli's political outlook: the concept of "crisis of the nation-state." This concept occupies in federalist theory the same place as the concept of "crisis of absolute monarchy" in liberal theory and the concept of "crisis of capitalism" in marxist theory. It enables us to identify the fundamental contradiction of our age, to formulate a comprehensive historical judgement on it and to provide a clear interpretation of the problems of our epoch based on new theoretical principles in comparison with traditional thinking. What Einaudi and the British federalist school showed was that the national form of the state was unable to cope with the basic trends in the course of history (internationalisation of the productive process, formation of a world system of states, supremacy of states with macroregional dimension). Furthermore, they pointed out the relationship between the crisis of the European states system and German imperialism, world wars, international economic disorder and the authoritarian degeneration of the structure of nation-states.

Spinelli in Switzerland

It was only when he became a political refugee in Switzerland shortly after the foundation of the European Federalist Movement in Italy (Milan, 27-28 August 1943) that Spinelli had free access to the British and American federalist literature in the library of the League of Nations in Geneva. There he completed his federalist education.

What inspired Spinelli's and Rossi's decision to migrate to Switzerland was the need to find other federalists in Europe, in order to be able to organise a federalist movement at European level and to initiate a common action for the United States of Europe. After 16 years of imprisonment, Spinelli had no relationship with the other resistance movements in Europe. He compared himself to an astronomer, who simply by studying the disturbance of the orbit of the farthest planet, without scanning the sky with a telescope, was able to forecast the existence of a new planet.[11]

Spinelli was convinced that the resistance movements had drawn the same lesson from fascism and war and had elaborated similar plans for the reorganisation of Europe in a federal form; that the common commitment for European federation could not be pursued without a common political organisation; and that the overcoming of national borders, conceived as the boundaries of political action, represented an absolute necessity for federalists. In 1944 Spinelli and Rossi succeeded in organising a conference of representatives of European resistance and liberation movements from nine countries which adopted two declarations: a statement of solidarity with the movements fighting against Nazism, and a manifesto for the United States of Europe. In spite of the difficulties in communications during the war, the resistance leaders succeeded in circulating their ideas all over Europe. This meeting represented a step towards the organisation of a federalist movement at European level, which was to occur in 1946 in Paris. The federalist organisations of most European countries joined this movement (the UEF).

During their stay in Switzerland, Spinelli and Rossi kept in touch with Einaudi, who was, as we have seen, the vehicle for the dissemination of British federalist literature at Ventotene. It must be noted that Einaudi was familiar with this literature. It is sufficient to read the bibliography at the end of his book entitled *La guerra e l'unità europea (War and European Unity)* to perceive how ample was his knowledge of that political and economic tradition.[12] Spinelli recalls in his memoirs the encounter between Rossi and Einaudi in Geneva. When Rossi recollected the role of the *Political Letters* of Junius as the foundation stone of the federalist outlook elaborated in Ventotene, Einaudi stated that, in the meanwhile, his interest had shifted to the functionalist theory of the Romanian economist David Mitrany, who just in 1943 had written a book entitled *A Working Peace System* and published by the Royal Institute of International Affairs in London.[13] It is to be noted that Mitrany was not only a functionalist, but also an antifederalist.

Einaudi acknowledged that this choice was a consequence of the fact that the message he had launched at the end of World War One had "remained unheeded and he himself had almost forgotten it. But he was clearly struck by the encounter with a man who had listened to it and was working for its dissemination. He was fascinated by Rossi and promised him to commit himself again to follow that way, kept his word and we benefited from his precious support till the end of his life."[14] His federalist commitment started during his stay in Switzerland where, as noted in his diary, he attended several meetings of federalist refugees belonging to the resistance movements of France, Germany, the Netherlands and Yugoslavia. As a result of those discussions he came to the conclusion that "The best project was the English one of Federal Union."[15] As a matter of fact, as regards Federal Union's influence on Spinelli, Richard Mayne and John Pinder wrote: "When Federal Union's members examined the Manifesto, they were especially pleased to find that it echoed some of the language they had used in documents of their own."[16]

The longer we observe Spinelli's activities after his release, the more evident becomes the distance which separates him from Einaudi, whose little book written 20 years earlier had revealed the main features of federalist theory. In Einaudi's works no political proposal on how to carry out the federalist design can be found. Once he had illustrated the nature of the objective to be pursued, he considered his task accomplished. After all, this was also the limit to Rossi's political outlook. Anyone who reads his most important essay on European federalism, *Gli Stati Uniti d'Europa (The United States of Europe)*,[17] published in Switzerland in 1944, can remark that his masterly illustration of the historical and political reasons for European unification is not associated with any reflection on the action which is necessary to pursue that objective.

Spinelli's theory of action

It is in the field of political action that Spinelli's role has a really innovatory significance in comparison with all previous federalist experience. The *Ventotene Manifesto* represents the starting point in the development of a new field of federalist thinking: a theory of democratic action for uniting a group of sovereign states. I think that in Spinelli's theory of action we can identify five guiding principles:

The current relevance of the European federation, which is no longer conceived as a distant ultimate goal, but as a political programme of a new generation of politicians who have learnt the lesson of world wars.

The strategic priority of the objective of European federation as compared with reform of nation-states, which represents a reversal of the order of priorities inspiring the conduct of political parties.

The shift of focus of political struggle from the national to the international level, implying a new cleavage between progressive and conservative forces – no longer identified as between liberalism and socialism but rather between nationalism and federalism.

The construction of a new independent federalist force (the European Federalist Movement), conceived as the vehicle for the struggle for the European federation. More precisely the consent of public opinion to the federalist project can enable the European Federalist Movement to push national governments to transfer their sovereignty to a European level.

Only a European constituent assembly can frame the European federal institutions which cannot spring from intergovernmental negotiations.

The progress of ideas, if it is to be a true progress, depends on co-operation amongst those who seek a solution to the problems of humanity. It is a collective effort of many participating in a common undertaking: the improvement of the conditions of political life. This means that reason is the element that connects the several phases of human history, links past to future generations and enlightens the march of humanity in history. This reflection on the nature of progress applies also to Spinelli. He did not start from scratch. The Founding Fathers of the United States of America, the reformers of the Commonwealth, the promoters of Federal Union had addressed similar problems and made an attempt to find a solution to them. This is the framework in which British federalists' influence on him should be studied.

Even though, on the whole, it is more appropriate to speak of a mutual influence between British federalists and Spinelli, initially Spinelli's federalist choice, as he himself acknowledges, was largely influenced by the British literature. That was the main source of his federalist learning. But, as soon as he had absorbed the fundamental principles of federalist theory, he became the founder of the movement for European unity. Spinelli's theory of federalist action, whose first formulation is contained in the *Ventotene Manifesto*, transformed federalism, which, until then, was placed in the world of ideas, into an action programme of an international political movement going far beyond the effective political action of federal union in the years 1938-40.

The constituent assembly

Let us consider, by way of example, one of Spinelli's most characteristic political proposals: the European constituent assembly. Although the concept of constituent assembly is foreign to the constitutional history of Britain and the British people never had any experience of such a method for building institution, the application of this idea to the construction of federal institutions developed first during the discussions on federal reform of the British Empire. Indeed, Lionel Curtis maintained that the habit of viewing constitutional change in British history as a gradual process is not in keeping with the facts.

The main assumption on which Curtis based his theory of constitutional change is that changes necessary to effect in order to transform the commonwealth into a federation "must all be realized together and simultaneously by passing a constitutional statute."[18] In Curtis's opinion, "there can be no intermediate period" during which the governments of the Dominions and the Commonwealth can co-exist. The birth of the British constitution shows that: "The Union of England and Scotland ... was consummated by means of a 'cut-and-dried' plan, and could not possibly have been effected in any other way. It was 'cut' in the shape of articles discussed and agreed upon by English and Scottish Commissioners appointed for that purpose in 1706, and by them drafted into the form of a Bill, which in 1707 was 'dried' or perpetuated as a legal enactment by the Scottish and English Parliaments... A brand-new state was created by an instrument of government deliberately devised and consciously adopted by the two Parliaments; and each, in doing so, effaced itself. This instrument was the written constitution of the new state they brought into existence; and its character as a written constitution is in no way altered by the fact that it has since become overlaid by a mass of subsequent usages and enactments. In no other way could a voluntary union have been effected."

On the other hand, Curtis asserted the necessity of popular consent in the procedure which is adopted for drafting the constitution. The historical experience brings ample evidence that this is a general tendency. In the United States "in 1787 the states appointed delegates who met at Philadelphia, framed a constitution, and submitted it for acceptance or refusal by the people of each state." In Canada "delegates from all the provinces met at Quebec in October 1864 and framed a series of resolutions, which were then submitted for approval to each of their legislatures. When adopted by the provinces, 'the resolutions were embodied in a Bill, to which legal effect was given in 1867 by an Act of the Imperial Parliament' ." In Australia "a series of Conventions produced a series of drafts, the last Convention completing its work in 1898. The scheme was then submitted by the parliaments of each colony in the form of a carefully drafted Bill to the electors themselves." In South Africa "the same procedure was followed so far as Natal was concerned. In the other colonies the scheme for union was accepted by each parliament without a referendum or direct election."

Curtis's second assumption is that "The Convention is the procedure necessary for the expression of public opinion... A Convention... is... essential to the principle of government by public opinion. Any attempt to settle such questions without first holding a Convention means that politicians are manoeuvring either to avoid a settlement or to make one behind the backs of the electorates." It is well known that the outbreak of World War One shattered the dream of a closer union of the Commonwealth. Nationalism, the poisoned fruit generated by war, brought about the disruption of all multinational empires. The federalist alternative to the organisation of the world into sovereign states was not yet ripe.

In conclusion, it is to be noted that the historical evolution of European integration represents a refutation of Curtis's opinion on the transition of a system of independent communities from division to unity. Although European integration has lasted longer than half a century and has created powerful institutions such as a European Parliament directly elected and endowed with legislative powers, a European Central Bank and a single currency, it is still an unaccomplished process. It began in 1951 with the European Coal and Steel Community and has not yet come to an end even with the Lisbon Reform Treaty, which maintains the right of national veto in crucial matters such as fiscal, foreign, security and defence policies and constitutional revision procedure. In other words, the Reform Treaty perpetuates the subordination of the European Union to national governments in the above mentioned matters.

At the beginning, Spinelli followed Curtis's model. He progressively departed from it, since he perceived that the unification of Europe was developing according to the method of constitutional gradualism, which has led to the bestowal of exclusive competences (commercial and fisheries policies and customs union) to the European Community, to the direct election of the European Parliament, to the monetary union and now to the Reform Treaty. Nonetheless, Spinelli remained faithful to the idea of the constituent assembly, conceived as the necessary procedure to be adopted in order to associate the people of two or more communities in the framing of the Constitution establishing a common government. Conventions, which drew up the Charter of Fundamental Rights in 2000 and the Draft Constitution in 2002-3, represent a confirmation of the need to associate the representatives of the peoples in the constitutional process and to withdraw from the governments the monopoly of decision-making power over constitutional matters.

Federalism as a political priority: the difference between Spinelli and Rossi

For Spinelli, federalism was a political priority. It was not simply an adjunct (or an accessory) to liberalism, as it was for his teachers – Einaudi and Robbins – or to socialism, as it was for Barbara Wootton. Spinelli regarded federalism as a real political alternative to Europe's organisation in sovereign states. Unlike political parties (and traditional ideologies inspiring them) which generally continue to confine themselves to plan government or regime changes within state borders, but do not question their own state, the federalist project aims at a more radical change, which affects the very nature of the state, i.e. its transformation into a member state of a federation. For Spinelli federalism is the response to the greatest problems of contemporary society, which have acquired much wider dimensions than nation-states. The federalist outlook is the expression of the awareness that the European unification and the unification of other great regions of the world in the perspective of world unity, have the priority over the goal of renewing individual states considered separately.

Federalism is "a canon for the interpretation of politics."[19] In a passage of his diary Spinelli enunciates this important definition of federalism. The adoption of this point of view enables us to distinguish Spinelli's from Rossi's approach to federalism. In Spinelli's opinion, Rossi "did not even suspect" that this could be the nature of federalism. Rossi conceives federalism simply as a method for the organisation of power, a constitutional technique which abolishes armed conflicts among states which have subscribed to a federal pact. In other words, federation appears as an alternative to war and not the response to the main problems of the current phase of history characterised by the historical crisis of the nation-state. Conceived in these terms, federalism is simply the completion of liberalism and socialism, a means to protect the values promoted by these ideologies from the negative consequences of international anarchy. In comparison with Spinelli, Rossi's adherence to federalism had a weaker motivation. The practical consequence of this standpoint was Rossi's giving up of the European Federalist Movement after the fall of the European Defence Community in 1954, when, owing to the thawing of the Cold War, the danger of a Third World War began to lessen.

The political itinerary of Lionel Robbins

Lionel Robbins's political journey shows similarities to Rossi's. The realisation that a truly international economy required an international rule of law led Robbins to advocate a global federal order. "There is world economy. But there is no world polity," he wrote in *Economic Planning and International Order*.[20] This was why international politics was still at the mercy of the brutish law of the "state of nature." Robbins concluded that a federal framework should be applied to the world. In *The Economic Causes of War* he developed his ideas in order to show the limits of the marxist theory of imperialism and to present federalism as the solution to the problem of war, which in fact broke out in September 1939 while he was concluding the final chapter of this book. Entitled "The Ultimate Cause of International Conflict", it was a passionate peroration for the United States of Europe. Here he clarified his position on the relationship between world and European federalism. The second objective represented, at that time, his first priority. He qualified "utopian" a federation of world dimensions, since "there is not sufficient feeling of a common citizenship," there is "no sufficiently generalized culture" and "even the electoral problems of such a body would present insurmountable difficulties."[21] We could add another outstanding difficulty, which was still present after the world wars, especially during the Cold War, namely the deep cleavages which were dividing the states in the international system. Of course, a world federation is "the divine event towards which all that is good in the heritage of the diverse civilizations of the world, invites us to strive." But it is a distant ultimate goal of human history.

On the contrary, in Robbins's opinion, it is not utopian to strive for more limited federations. In particular in Europe the economic and technological evolution was imposing the overcoming of national sovereignties. "As gunpowder rendered obsolete the feudal system," Robbins wrote, "so the aeroplane renders obsolete the system of the independent sovereignties of Europe." He concluded with this cogent argument: "A more comprehensive type of organization is inevitable. Will it come by mutual agreement or by caesarian conquest? That is the unsolved question. For either there must be empire or federation; on a long view, there is no alternative."

The war had shown how obsolete was the organisation of Europe into nation-states. There was no alternative to the European union. What remained undetermined was the way that goal could be reached. The choice was between an empire in the European continent under German rule or a federation including a democratic Germany. Churchill's proposal for a Franco-British Union in June 1940 represents the extraordinary convergence between a government position and federalist ideas, which had found in Federal Union its organised expression. This failed attempt to follow a new way - a federalist way - can be explained only by the war and the desperate struggle for life which Britain was facing. Jean Monnet[22] was the author of Churchill's plan. When France was occupied by the Nazi army, he was in London, where he was president of the Franco-British committee for organising joint purchasing of war supplies. Monnet's special talent lay in his capacity to influence crucial decisions, working far from the limelight, in the background where the future is prepared patiently.

Aside from that episode, Churchill always pursued UK independence. In a 1930 article, with that beautiful concise expression, which is a special quality of the English language, he had stated: "We have our own dream... We are with Europe, but not of it."[23] In other words, Churchill envisaged European integration only for the countries of the Continent, not for Britain. This is the fundamental meaning of the message he launched from the University of Zürich in 1946, when he supported again the idea of "a kind of United States of Europe," but keeping for Britain the role of a sponsor from the outside. For him, a united Europe was first of all the necessary bulwark against Soviet expansionism.

Unlike Lord Lothian, another towering exponent of British federalism, who died in 1940 during World War Two, Robbins lived until 1984. Thus, he witnessed the development of European unification until the direct election of the European Parliament. He never repudiated either the idea of the decline of the nation-states or his attachment for the concept of federalism. What is paradoxical is the fact that Robbins, who had been one of the most brilliant advocates of European federalism, gave up this specific cause just at the moment, after the war, when the political conditions for European unification were ripening. In his autobiography he wrote that: "When the United Europe movement was first launched in the shape of proposals for the Coal and Steel Community, I opposed it. I opposed it, not because I had in any way abandoned my desire for the creation of larger units, but rather because I thought that the creation of this larger unit ran the danger of being inimical to the creation of a still larger one, or at any rate to forms of political and economic co-operation over a wide area which were essential if the Western world were not to fall apart."[24] The larger unit to which Robbins was referring was the Atlantic Community.

Robbins wrote that during the war he "became more and more convinced of the indispensability of continued American co-operation in maintaining the balance of the world. In two world wars the nations of Europe had not succeeded in solving their problems unaided." Consequently, "a continuation, in some form or other, of political and military association between ourselves and the two great unions of North America seemed to me to be the *sine qua non* for any hope of preserving the civilization of the West." One reason for his disenchantment with the European federalist cause was the anti-Americanism characterising the attitudes of many intellectuals and politicians especially in France.[25]

In a speech at the UEF founding congress in 1947 Spinelli affirmed that the recently launched Marshall Plan had provided "an opportunity that the European democracies must grasp and turn to their advantage. However, all the Americans can do on these lines is to offer us the opportunity. They can accept the formation of a peaceful and prosperous European union... But they cannot themselves create such a union, and, if the Europeans cannot seize the opportunity, the US will be more and more tempted to move from the liberal alternative to that of imperialism. This latter alternative is strong in America; it develops in parallel with the former one, and it is this which makes every American initiative and intervention of such crucial importance for us. If democratic Europe does not save itself by its own efforts, making use of the American opportunity, and does not develop federal institutions in the economic and political fields, then it is American imperialism that will prevail."[26] Spinelli immediately understood that the Marshall Plan offered a unique opportunity to take an initiative for the European economic and political union within the Western block, so as to create the conditions for an equal partnership between Europe and America. Otherwise, the political division of Europe would have inevitably promoted American imperialism.

It was only in 1960 that Robbins admitted his mistake[27] when the extraordinary success of the European Community had shown that the root of European integration was the decline of nation-states. Its historical significance lay in the overcoming of the contradiction between the scale of the major problems and the size of the nation-states, which he had indeed already identified in his two books in the 1930s that had so much influence on Spinelli. Instead, the cohesion of the Atlantic alliance was dependent on the hegemony of the United States. At the same time, the unsuccessful Suez expedition had degraded Britain to a second-class position in the hierarchy of world powers and the dream of the maritime mission was approaching sunset. Hence the British decision to make the application for membership of the European Community.

This state of uncertainty with regard to the European federation shows that Robbins failed to realise that a successful development of federalism through European unification was in fact essential for the prevalence of pluralist democracy in Europe, rather than authoritarian Soviet communism. Nor did he, for all his merits, realise that European unification has the significance of a first step in the unification of the world, albeit beginning in a part of that world. The fact is that he did not conceive the European federation as a political priority, stemming from a new political thinking, as suggested by the *Ventotene Manifesto*.

The rise and decline of Federal Union
Robbins's political journey represents one individual aspect of a wider collective phenomenon: the rise and decline of Federal Union. Between 1938 and 1940 the movement played a leading role in promoting the federal design and exerted a real influence on Churchill's proposal to the French government to create a Franco-British Union: the first federalist project promoted by a national government in the history of Europe. It is uncertain how many members joined Federal Union – estimates vary between 10-60 thousand: by 1940 there were no fewer than 253 local branches. The movement was supported by so many distinguished people that Mayne and Pinder are able to claim that "the establishment" gave it its backing [28]. Moreover, the fact that 100,000 copies of Curry's *The Case for Federal Union* were sold after the outbreak of war shows the extraordinary impact that the movement had on British public opinion. The action of Federal Union was so penetrating that it can "claim, with some justification," wrote Charles Kimber, "to have brought the offer of union with France within the 'art of the possible' (at least in that desperate moment). But it also can claim to have put federation at the top of the agenda of such public discussion of 'war aims' as Churchill's insistence on 'unconditional surrender' allowed."[29]

While the Federal Union Research Institute, created by William Beveridge to discuss the significance of, and make proposals relating to, a European federation, survived the war and became Federal Trust, Federal Union's branches and the organisation suffered severely. In spite of that, as Mayne and Pinder write, "Federal Union had been the prime mover in creating the international federalist movements at both European and world level."[30] After the war the organisation remained with some 2,000 members. However, most of the key figures were no longer active, though Beveridge became a very efficient and energetic President and Mackay was to carry on his federalist campaign in Parliament rather than in Federal Union.

Many did not realise that the political framework within which to build the future was Europe. Some federalists chose the political commitment at national level as their priority, some chose other priorities: Atlantic community, world federation and so forth. It was the need to prevent war by means of a federal government above the states that had allowed British public opinion to unite above party lines. But when the war was over, the divisions across party lines prevailed again. However, it is worth mentioning that in 1948 Mackay was able to secure about a hundred signatures from both Labour and Conservative MPs for a motion calling for a constituent assembly to design a European federal constitution, in keeping with Spinelli's ideas.[31]

Federal Union represents a milestone in the history of federalism: the first example of a federalist movement made up of a group of active members capable of exerting an influence on public opinion and "the establishment," i.e. political, intellectual and social circles, organised over the territory with local branches and a newsletter. This organisational model is not substantially different from that applied by post-war federalist movements.

The post-war period

After World War Two commitment to a European federation appeared much more difficult in Britain than in some other countries of Western Europe. Six countries on the Continent assumed leadership of the process of European unification, while Britain refused to participate in the European Community. The crisis of the sovereign state was slower to become evident in the British Isles than on the Continent. Unlike France, Britain did not suffer the humiliation of a Nazi invasion and was able to keep alive until after the Suez crisis the dream of a world role among the big powers.

This means that the first attempt at constructing the European federation led by Spinelli in the post-war period occurred within the framework of the six founding countries of the European Community without the participation of Britain. It matured in the early fifties following Monnet's initiative to found the European Coal and Steel Community (ECSC) as a European framework for the reconstruction of Germany. Spinelli's intervention ensured that the next initiative - to create a European Defence Community (EDC) - was accompanied by a constituent process in which the ad hoc Assembly (the enlarged ECSC Assembly) was given a mandate to draw up the statute of the European Political Community (EPC), the political body needed to control the European army. It was Spinelli's federalist outlook which enabled him to realise that the European army had to be responsible to a federal government. His political genius enabled him to convince Italian Prime Minister De Gasperi of this and it was the latter who persuaded the governments of the other member states to agree to draft the treaty for the EPC to accompany the EDC. It is worth recalling that the EPC would have been only partially federal in nature, since it maintained a number of intergovernmental structures and procedures. The process was abruptly halted in 1954, when the French National Assembly rejected the EDC after four out of six member states of the European Community had already ratified it.

When the European Union of Federalists split after the failure of the EDC, the British federalists chose to join the Action Européenne Fédéraliste (AEF), which supported the European Community, as a step toward a European federation, while Spinelli launched within the Mouvement Fédéraliste Européen (MFE) the campaign for the Congress of the European People and focused its action for the constituent assembly.

In spite of the weakening of political influence of British federalists in their country, their intellectual contribution to federalism remains highly relevant. It is sufficient to mention the classic book of Kenneth C. Wheare on *Federal Government* [32] published in 1946, a comparative analysis on the four federations (United States, Switzerland, Canada and Australia) existing at the time. It remains a point of reference for every scholar of federal institutions. Another example is the distinction drawn by John Pinder in 1968 between "negative" and "positive" integration,[33] which has become a part of the language generally utilised to speak of the subject. It provides an essential instrument for distinguishing the stages of European integration. He called the first stage negative because it comprised the elimination of the obstacles to the free circulation of goods, services, capital and labour, but the second stage positive, since it expressed the need to promote common European policies in the areas of social and regional development, the environment, external trade, currency and foreign and security relations.

The most important contribution of the post-war British federalist school lies in the idea that the construction of the European federation is a gradual process in which both economic and institutional steps forward are closely intertwined. The relevance of this approach becomes evident if we take into account that in 1957 Spinelli published an article entitled 'The Common Market Mockery' [34] in which he maintained that the objective of the treaty establishing the EEC could not be achieved without a European government. This means that at the very beginning of the process of

European economic integration Spinelli's guiding idea was that a European government should be conceived as the point of departure in the construction of the European federation. Of course, in a few years' time Spinelli changed his mind. When he recognised the success of the Common Market, he began to view the European Community as the embryo of the European federation. "In a strange and precarious but unquestionable way Europe is coming into existence," he noted in his Diary in 1962.[35]

Spinelli's second attempt at constructing a European federation matured after the direct election of the European Parliament, of which he was a member. It highlights his changed opinion regarding the nature of the European Community. The opportunity was offered by the seeming contradiction of an elected parliament with little more than consultative powers. This made it possible to begin the struggle to confer the power to make laws and control the executive to the sovereign people through parliamentary representation. The latest incarnation of his particular idea of a constituent assembly is represented by the design of a constituent role for the European Parliament. Although in Spinelli's view his last battle failed, it is interesting to note that his objective was an intermediate step on the way towards the European federation. The Draft Treaty for European Union, approved by the European Parliament on 14 February 1984, proposed the creation of the conditions for strengthening the government of the European economy, but postponed the solution to the problem of the unification of foreign and security policy.

The fact is that the overcoming of the division of Europe into nation-states is a historical process, which cannot be compared with the unification of the United States of America. Any simple analogy is misleading. The unification of the 13 republics in North America was an easy and quick undertaking, because the member states had a homogeneous structure, were of small size and had trifling power in world politics. Instead, European unification entails the overcoming of deep divisions among states that are proud of their independence and have been divided by sharp conflicts and bloody wars throughout the course of centuries. This means that the European federation is not emerging (and cannot emerge) as a full-fledged state at once. The model of Philadelphia (a constitutional convention that framed the federal constitution in four months) suggests the idea that a qualitative leap can solve the problem of the transition from a confederation to a federation. It is not fit for the political unification of Europe.

It took nearly 15 years after the end of World War Two before Britain started to recognise that her future lay with Europe. The Suez crisis in 1956 was the starting point of a change of attitude toward Europe, since it showed that Britain was no longer a world power. Federalists realised that this was a good opportunity to enter the scene and campaign for Britain in Europe. But they had to face de Gaulle's double veto. The organisational and theoretical commitment of the British federalists led them to propose, during a conference of Federal Trust held in 1968, an ambitious plan, formulated by John Pinder, to convene a second Messina conference to create a European political community with the UK as a full member which would operate alongside the Economic Community, in order "to include foreign policy and security, defence technologies and monetary policy, with institutions that would become federal by the end of a transitional period."[36] George Brown, who had only recently resigned as Foreign Secretary, gave his backing and Spinelli gained the support of Pietro Nenni, who was on the point of becoming the Italian Foreign Minister. The initiative of Britain and Italy was overtaken by de Gaulle's resignation in 1969, which opened the door of the European Community to Britain. The campaign for EC membership, led by the Director of the European Movement, Ernest Wistrich [37] was a spectacular success. The federalists were again at the centre of the political scene.

The plan for the European Political Community was the starting point of a theoretical reflection enabling British federalists to elaborate a gradualist strategy for European unification combining Monnet's and Spinelli's approaches. Pinder reached the conclusion that "the constitutional federalism of Spinelli and functionalist federalism of Monnet can be seen to be complementary."[38] Michael Burgess reaches the same conclusions in his research on the influence of federalist ideas on the evolution of the European Community.[39] The evolution of the Italian federalists' thinking is convergent. Mario Albertini, the leader of the Italian branch of the UEF from the 'sixties to the 'nineties identified three strategic objectives: the direct election of the European Parliament, the Monetary Union and the Constitution, which have become the objectives of the UEF and then the stages of the institutional evolution of the European Union.[40]

There is widespread recognition that the European institutions, and more generally the process of European integration, have eliminated from our horizons a prospect that was the nightmare of past generations: the spectre of a war between France and Germany. It is significant that this occurred without and before the European federation. This is a relatively new achievement of federalist theory. But we can support this idea as long as the process of European unification, and particularly the perspective of a unification of foreign, security and defence policies, remains open. Even the gravity of the current crisis, due to the rejection of the European constitution by the French and the Dutch peoples, offers cause for optimism. Although imperfect and unaccomplished, the European democracy represents a mighty bulwark against the danger of disruption of the EU. Most politicians hoping for re-election know that public opinion would never forgive them for breaking up a community that has proved to be able to assure peace, prosperity and democracy to a growing number of countries.

The convergence between the British and the Italian federalist schools shows that the European federalists are now sharing common views on the nature of European unification and the strategy to achieve the European federation. All the founders of Federal Union, except Charles Kimber, and of the Movimento Federalista Europeo, are dead. Like Moses, they have died before reaching the Promised Land. It is up to the living generations to continue the path to its conclusion.

Notes to Chapter 3

[1] A. Spinelli, *Come ho tentato di diventare saggio* (Bologna: Il Mulino, 2006), pp. 257, p. 311.

[2] *Socialismo liberale* (1928) (Torino: Einaudi, 1979) is a seminal book of Carlo Rosselli, where he advocated democratic and liberal political institutions, a mixed economy, social justice and international peace.

[3] A. Spinelli, *op. cit.*, pp. 261 and 302.

[4] The reference of this book is Junius, *Lettere politiche* (Bari: Laterza, 1920). This book has never been reprinted. However, the most significant articles have been reproduced in: L. Einaudi, *La guerra e l'unità europea* (Milano: Comunità, 1948), reprinted several times in the post-war period.

[5] A. Spinelli, *op. cit.*, pp. 307-308.

[6] A. Spinelli, *Machiavelli nel secolo XX. Scritti del confino e della clandestinità. 1941-1944*, edited by Piero Graglia (Bologna: Il Mulino, 1993), pp. 522-533.

[7] J. Pinder (ed.), *Altiero Spinelli and the British Federalists* (London: Federal Trust, 1998), p. viii. On the same subject see also J. Pinder, 'Federalism in Britain and Italy: Radicals and the English Liberal Tradition', in P.M.R. Stirk (ed.), *European Unity in Context: The Interwar Period* (London: Pinter Publishers, 1989), pp. 201-223, reprinted in L. Levi (ed.), *Altiero Spinelli and Federalism in Europe and the World* (Milano: Angeli, 1990), pp. 85-110.

[8] A. Spinelli, E. Rossi, *The Ventotene Manifesto* (Ventotene: The Altiero Spinelli Institute for Federalist Studies, 1988).

[9] L. Robbins, *Autobiography of an Economist* (London: Macmillan, 1971), p. 160.

[10] E. Rossi claims the authorship of this translation in *Miserie e splendori del confino di polizia. Lettere da Ventotene. 1939-1943* (Milano: Feltrinelli, 1981), p. 149.

[11] A. Spinelli, *Come ho tentato di diventare saggio*, p. 370.

[12] See note 4.

[13] D. Mitrany, *A Working Peace System* (London: Oxford University Press, 1943).

[14] A. Spinelli, *Come ho tentato di diventare saggio*, p. 389.

[15] L. Einaudi, *Diario d'esilio. 1943-1944* (Torino: Einaudi, 1997), p. 140.

[16] R. Mayne, J. Pinder, *Federal Union: The Pioneers. A History of Federal Union* (London: Macmillan, 1990), p. 84.

[17] Storeno (pen name of E. Rossi), *Gli Stati Uniti d'Europa* (Lugano: Nuove Edizioni di Capolago, 1944). Anastatic reprint edited by S. Pistone (Torino: CELID, 2004).

[18] L. Curtis, *The Problem of the Commonwealth* (London: Macmillan, 1916), p. 222.

[19] A. Spinelli, *Diario europeo*, edited by Edmondo Paolini (Bologna: Il Mulino, 1989), Vol. I, p. 214.

[20] L. Robbins, *Economic Planning and International Order* (London: Macmillan, 1937), p. 239.

[21] L. Robbins, *The Economic Causes of War* (London: Jonathan Cape, 1939), p. 105.

[22] Monnet devotes the first chapter of his *Mémoires* (Paris: Fayard, 1976), pp. 13-36, to the narration of this event.

[23] W. Churchill, 'The United States of Europe', *Saturday Evening Post*, New York, 15 February, 1930, reproduced in R. Ducci, B. Olivi (eds), *L'Europa incompiuta* (Padova: CEDAM, 1970), p. 37.

[24] L. Robbins, *Autobiography of an Economist*, p. 238.

[25] *Ibid.*, p. 236. It is worth recollecting that in *The Economic Causes of War* Robbins upheld the opposite opinion, when he discussed Clarence Streit's proposal for a federation of the democracies, including the United States and the British Empire, in *Union Now* (New York and London: Harper and Brothers, 1939). In principle, he had no objection to the scheme: "The larger the federation, the smaller the area of future wars". But he thought that "It does not seem probable that, in our generation at least, the citizens of the United States will feel that compelling urge to union with other peoples which would alone make it possible" (p. 106).

[26] A. Spinelli, *Dagli Stati sovrani agli Stati Uniti d'Europa* (Firenze: La Nuova Italia, 1950), p. 234.

[27] During a speech delivered in Rome in the spring of 1960, entitled 'Liberalism and the International Problem' and published in *Politics and Economics* (London: Macmillan, 1963), pp. 154-155.

[28] R. Mayne and J. Pinder, *op. cit.*, p. 19.

[29] C. Kimber, 'The Birth of Federal Union', *The Federalist Debate*, XVIII, 2005, n. 1, p. 14.

[30] R. Mayne, J. Pinder, *op. cit.*, p. 54.

[31] *Ibid.*, p. 100.

[32] K. C. Wheare, *Federal Government* (Oxford: Oxford University Press, 1946).

33 J. Pinder, 'Positive Integration and Negative Integration: Some problems of Economic Union in the EEC', *The World Today*, XXIV, 1968, pp. 89-110.

34 A. Spinelli, *L'Europa non cade dal cielo* (Bologna: Il Mulino, 1960), pp. 282-287.

35 A. Spinelli, *Diario europeo*, p. 423.

36 R. Mayne, J. Pinder, *op. cit.*, p. 182.

37 E. Wistrich, 'The Federalist Struggle in Britain', *The Federalist*, XXVI, 1984, n. 3, pp. 230-240. See ch. 4 below.

38 J. Pinder, 'From Milan to Maastricht: Fifty Years of Federalist Struggle for the Uniting of Europe', *The Federalist*, XXXV, 1993, n. 3, p. 159.

39 M. Burgess, *Federalism and the European Union: Political Ideas, Influences and Strategies in the European Community. 1972-1987* (London and New York: Routledge, 1989).

40 J. Pinder, 'Mario Albertini in the History of Federalist Thought', *The Federalist*, XLIV, 2002, n. 3, pp. 157-170.

Envoi

Jean Monnet and Britain

Richard Mayne

WORKED WITH MONNET FROM 1956 PRACTICALLY UNTIL HIS
DEATH IN 1979. The topic given was "Monnet and Britain," but I
suppose in a federalist context I ought to address the question of
whether Monnet was a federalist. I don't think he would ever have called
himself a federalist and some people have claimed that he denied that he
was. Nonetheless, he certainly believed in rules and institutions. He
advocated federalism twice in the Schuman declaration of 1950 and he used
the word a dozen times in his memoirs. He believed that the nation-state
should not be the sole arbiter of the nation-state's affairs and that there
should be some supranational body to make sure that member states were
not judge and jury in their own causes all the time. The word "supranational"
is now, of course, rather a dead letter particularly in the thoughts of
Europeans who are afraid of the eurosceptics. Personally I don't mind the
word supranational as long as it's properly understood. It seemed at one time
to mean a body, a government above member states but let me quote what
Monnet himself said to me on one occasion, after the British referendum in
1975, when we had lunch together at Prunier's in Paris. An appropriate
English version is: "You know we were wrong in those days to say the
Community was supranational. What it really is, in practice, is a dialogue
between the member states and the Commission." That I think is, in a sense,
the essence of federalism as applied to the European Union.

Monnet was not a doctrinaire thinker. He was not a political philosopher,
but he had a great sense of two things: one, the ultimate objective, which
was always ultimate and the other the immediate task, which was always
immediate - "we must do it now." That combination which may seem to leave
out the medium term, was nevertheless very powerful. When, in the
Schuman Declaration of 1950, he talked about supranationality and breaking
with the past, what he wanted was to break the logjam of countries trying to
form old-fashioned alliances rather than creating anything new, anything
solid. I've always thought of that latter as an attempt to, as I used to do when
I was a child - stick a broken toy together by licking the bits. It stuck for a

while but it subsequently fell apart again. Monnet had been aware that organisations like the Council of Europe and even OECD were likely to fall apart under nationalist pressure unless there was something slightly stronger than just "lick" holding them together. What he essentially did was to call for a European High Authority - words which nobody uses now. The High Authority was modelled partly on the International Ruhr Authority because the Coal and Steel Community was designed to replace the Ruhr Authority and its unilateral control on German heavy industry with a joint control over heavy industry in Germany, France and whichever other countries would want to join. So the High Authority - an extraordinarily difficult term for the British - was an attempt to break with the past, do something dramatic and change people's minds. That was the first occasion after the war when the British were in Monnet's sights.

I say post-war because he'd done something else with the British: indeed, he'd done several things with the British. When he was 16 (he never went to university - he had the great advantage of not undergoing higher education in France) he went to stay with a wine merchant in the City of London and he learnt his English there. Although later he spoke English with a slight American accent, English was his first foreign language - not American. That was his first contact with the British and from it he gained a great respect for something which has perhaps now disappeared - that is the unspoken bargain, the handshake, the gentleman's agreement. He lived in that world, he was already in that world of the gentleman's agreement. Very attractive, I think. He always stayed when he was in England at the Hyde Park Hotel, which was the embodiment of that Edwardian world, and he always had his clothes made in Savile Row. They were worn so hard that they didn't look it. He used to wear a terrible old overcoat which he'd had for years and years and years and which looked as if it had come off a scarecrow, but it was still very well cut. On the other hand, he was always travelling by chauffeur-driven car and he liked to travel first class. He had that sort of Edwardian cigar-smoking atmosphere about him and of course he drank his own brandy - his own firm's brandy - until quite late in life when he was asked, or advised, by his doctors that he shouldn't drink very much. He never became a drunkard or anything like that but he liked the good life and he deserved the good life and he'd been accustomed to it and it was part of his normal way of living. He felt that that was British. I remember also that he said of the British that, "once they've joined the Common Market they'll think they've invented it." He believed that the British understood rules and institutions in a way that perhaps the French and certainly the Italians did not. So he felt that the British presence in the European Union would be a strengthening, enhancing, educative thing.

He tried in 1940 to form a Franco-British union at the time when France was falling; Pétain had not yet arrived; the French government was taking refuge in Bordeaux. Monnet persuaded those two old romantic nationalists, Churchill and de Gaulle, to propose Anglo-French union because he thought this was the way not only to keep the French in the war but also, specifically, to keep the French fleet in the war. That certainly appealed to Churchill. Monnet also saw the concept of union as something that could be built on, after the war. Other people, including Vansittart, had the same idea, but it was Monnet who managed to persuade these two great figures, France's de Gaulle and Britain's Churchill, to endorse it. Churchill was all set to go out and sell it to the French but then came the news that the French government had fallen and that Reynaud had been dismissed. Monnet himself took a flying boat out to Bordeaux to try to bring back those members of the French government who would still agree to his scheme. None of them would and all he did was bring back a few refugees. He had a rather dispiriting time but the whole episode showed the fact that Monnet always felt that the British were an essential part of his scheme.

When the European Coal and Steel Community was proposed by Robert Schuman, but on a text by Monnet, the latter tried very, very hard to get the British in from the start. There was a long exchange of telegrams, which you can read in the archives, between the Quai D'Orsay and the Foreign Office, in which attempts were made to persuade the British to join the Community. However, the British would not accept a degree of supranationality. There was a long argument about it but finally they thought that no, it was not possible. Despite this, Monnet was still keen to get the British interested in the Coal and Steel Community and as a result he recruited an old friend of mine, now dead unfortunately, François Duchêne, to work as his liaison with the British. When François had to go back to Paris after Monnet left the High Authority, I was recruited to replace him, so in a sense I was a sort of second string in that game. The idea had always been in Monnet's mind that the British had a role in Europe and even before the Coal and Steel Community he had tried in 1949 to persuade the British to engage in joint planning. He had been head of the French Plan which was no more than indicative planning: it was certainly not Crippsian control planning. Monnet tried to persuade the British to take part in joint planning, but unfortunately it was the same old story. The British understood what was being offered as an attempt to exchange beef for coal and not to engage in a joint operation of looking at economies and deciding what should be done. That wasn't on the British map, or the British mental map, at that time. Monnet had failed back in 1940 when the French were in no state to respond, and again in 1949 and 1950 when the British wouldn't join the Coal and Steel Community. However, he never lost the feeling that Britain had a role in what he was trying to do.

Long afterwards when the British had already attempted to join and de Gaulle had twice vetoed them, Monnet was engaged in preparing his memoirs. It was a long and difficult process. Monnet's memoirs are not full of juicy anecdotes. I could tell you many. Example: Monnet was staying at the Hyde Park Hotel going out for his morning walk long before the Night Porter had gone off duty and coming back dressed in rather shabby, old clothes presenting himself at the desk when the Day Porter had arrived. For a moment he was turned away because they couldn't understand how this tramp wanted to come and sleep in the Hyde Park Hotel. That was typical of Monnet's behaviour even when he was in London. I remember another occasion when he was in London and my wife, Jocelyn, was there with him walking through Leicester Square, which was full of jazzy, snazzy, horrible things going on; Monnet looked around. "I hate this," he said, "I hate it." He was a man of strong feelings and had great nostalgia for the old Britain. He didn't much care for the new Britain. I don't know whether he would like the even newer Britain of today, but that is another story.

Monnet's memoirs are not full of that sort of thing. They were based on very careful research. He had most of his own archives, not all of them: there was one locked trunk to which nobody had the key and most of the old archives had been burnt by his family during the war because of fear of the German occupation, but he got a lot of people to write on various aspects of his life. I remember Jean-Baptiste Duroselle, the French historian, writing a piece about his relations with America. Another was on his work in Algeria during the war. Monnet asked me to write a piece (it turned out to be a book: it always does) on his relations with Great Britain because he was very keen to dispel any notion that he had built the foundations of Europe against the British. Some people alleged (and there are one or two historians who like alleging this kind of thing) that both Monnet and Schuman really wanted to keep the British out. It wasn't true even of Schuman who was a Catholic. Monnet was Catholic but he wasn't all that Catholic and he certainly wasn't anti-British or anti-Protestant. Monnet was very keen to dispel any illusion that he had not favoured the British.

What was very interesting was that during the whole of the first Heath negotiations from 1961 to 1963, when they were broken off by de Gaulle, Monnet was working behind the scenes as a kind of unspoken, unseen emissary between Britain, France and Brussels. I remember he used to stay in a hotel which was very like the Hyde Park Hotel. I remember being there with him when General de Gaulle had just vetoed the British. The German delegate in the negotiations had tears in his eyes. We were all shocked and horrified. I said to Monnet, "C'est déprimant" and he said, "Non, c'est attristant." The distinction was very important to him. It was saddening but it wasn't depressing because "I'm never disappointed," he used to say sometimes in a very disappointed voice. He was very disappointed that de Gaulle had vetoed the British but even then he proposed yet another attempt to get the British in by means of some nuclear deal with Heath and de Gaulle. He proposed to Heath that he should make an offer of Polaris to de Gaulle. Well it was pretty clear that it wouldn't work: a) because de Gaulle was too proud; b) because de Gaulle didn't want the British in and c) because a bilateral deal of that kind would have upset the Germans. However, it was an attempt by Monnet, which Heath began to look at, to rescue the British from the de Gaulle veto. When the second attempt came, the Wilson attempt to join, which was quickly vetoed by de Gaulle, Monnet continued to be very, very keen on Britain coming in.

After 1963 I was working for the Commission in London, but I was still very much in contact with Monnet and it was absolutely clear he was trying hard, mainly through Ted Heath, to persuade the British that at some point they must knock on the door again. As we know they did and Pompidou let them join. Monnet was very close to Pompidou's private office at that time and I am sure he gave Pompidou the right kind of advice. My own feeling about Monnet was that he had a slightly idealised and rather old-fashioned view of the British. As I said, he liked the old Edwardian style, he liked the gentleman's agreement; he liked the British for their respect for institutions. Accepting his own comment of never being disappointed, would he perhaps have been slightly disappointed by the way in which the British have failed to exploit and to fulfil their destiny in the European Union? Tony Blair made at least one very good speech about Europe, not in Whitehall but in Warsaw - not exactly the right place to do it. But he has never fulfilled in the European Union the sort of promise people thought he embodied when he came to power. I'm not making any criticism of Blair as an internal statesman or even Blair as the follower of Bush into the Iraq war. However, I feel sure that Monnet would have been very disappointed by that and more disappointed still by the fact that the British didn't make common cause with their European partners when it came to discussing the preliminaries of the Iraq war and when they didn't join the euro. He would also have been disappointed when the British failed to join the Schengen Agreement and when they failed to endorse with enthusiasm the idea of a European Constitution.

Now the European Constitution is, of course, a matter which many people think is dead. I don't think it is. I think there is quite a lot of sense in the Constitutional Treaty and I suspect that a lot of it is going to be revived. The real problem is calling it a constitution. I don't think Monnet would have used that word because in France a constitution is something you have and change. It's like a menu. You have a menu one day and another menu the next day and a third menu on the third day and so on. For the British the word "constitution" tends to be something which has been fixed forever, settled, and is not even written down. It might have been better to rename the Constitutional Treaty, the "Reform Treaty" or the "Adjustment Treaty" or the "Enlargement Treaty" or something else which could have conveyed to everybody that it was intended to adjust, and improve the working of, the institutions for 25 or 27 instead of 15 countries and not trying to lay down the basis, in the British perception, of a new constitution to supersede the one that they didn't have. That would have been, I am sure, Monnet's view - you do not want to frighten people with words: rather you want to confront them with facts. He always believed that the British were not convinced by ideas or by words, but when facts changed they would adjust. To some extent that is the way in which the British have talked about federalism. They have reacted reluctantly and as latecomers. Now that a federal system has been set up in Europe the British do not want to be left out. Monnet always knew that the British did not want to be left out and he felt that if you created something, they would then want to join. That is what has happened. But it has not made them, in the way that Monnet and his colleagues were, dynamic proponents of the idea - dynamic drivers toward the goal. To that extent it is a disappointment to me as well as it would have been to him.

A lot of people ask me what would Monnet be saying about Europe at the present time. As of the summer of 2006, I think he would be saying first of all we cannot do very much until the French elections are behind us, until

Prodi's position in Italy is either confirmed or destroyed and, maybe, until the Grand Coalition in Germany proves or disproves itself. We are in flux, in a sort of interim position – a difficult interval to live through. We have to live through it, but for the moment we cannot see very clearly who is leading, who is going to lead the major players on the European scene. Monnet, I think, would recognise that and would not expect anything very spectacular to happen in the next couple of years. However, he would surely still be pressing to go ahead on the work that has been done. I think he would recognise this even if Europe has lost the initial impulse we had when we were trying to bury the hatchet and stop trying to kill each other. We decided to stop doing that. We don't now have, in most of the population, memories of the war, memories of Hitlerism, memories of fascism. As a result we no longer feel the same impulsion to turn our backs on a savage past. We are in what seems to be a much more tranquil European world and to that extent we have to rely on the impetus of the institutions, and what exists, to replace the passion that ignited the whole thing at the beginning. I think Monnet would be convinced that this was OK because he really believed that men die but institutions survive. The institutions have not been gnawed away, but they have been surviving in difficult times. Even when de Gaulle was vetoing the British and when he played the empty chair policy, the institutions survived time, and we have had them now for 50 years and more. But we have to rely on them to help us carry on as a sort of heavy weight, like a flywheel on an engine, to keep it going at a time when the impulse from the accelerator is perhaps not what it should be. Monnet would rely on that and be quite happy about it.

I also think that Monnet would not be talking just about Europe in itself. He would be talking about the global challenges that we face which are not just economic and commercial, not just cheap Chinese shoes, but the challenges of climate change, of Islamists rather than Islam, and the poverty in parts of the world that we now know about but which we happily ignored for so many years. He would be concerned, as he always was, with world problems and not just European problems. What he would say, I think, is that if we seriously want to attack and deal with these problems, we cannot do it on a national basis - Britain cannot do it; France cannot do it. We have to do it as Europe and even Europe cannot do it alone. Europe has to forge alliances - self-respecting and mutually critical alliances as with the United States. I think Monnet would be very, very hesitant about the policies of the current US administration. He was very much against Goldwater when he was running for office. When he was defeated I remember Monnet saying, "Well, that just shows that the Americans have a great fund of common sense." I don't know if he would say that now for he would certainly be very critical of what has been done in Iraq and what is being done in Afghanistan. I think he would feel that unilateral action is not really conducive to world peace. He would be very concerned about the challenge to our values from the fundamentalists of every stripe. Every kind of fundamentalist would be anathema to Monnet and he would want Europe to ally with the sane people in the rest of the world to try to improve relations between the continents. There again, I say the continents because we have to consider India, we have to consider Brazil and China and we have to try to create out of those countries that are willing to do it something more like a consensus. It is not going to be easy, it is not going to be quick, it will never be complete, but it will be something better than what we have at the moment.

The only instrument that we British have in our hands to do this - and Monnet would say it - is Europe. We can't do it alone. We have to do it with Europe. I think if there were a tinge of disappointment in Monnet's mind at the moment, it would be that the British missed one opportunity to line up with their European partners to have a serious dialogue with the United States about foreign policy. Let them not miss another. Let them not engage in other adventures, which may be attractive but are very dangerous. I think he would probably say it is much easier to deal with Condoleezza Rice than it was to deal with Bush Mark I. Bush Mark II does seem to be changing a little bit. It may be that the civilian pressure of the European Union on various aspects of American policy including Guantanamo is having some effect on the American administration but it is quite clear that not one single European country acting alone could have done that. Monnet would be pleased to have 25 countries in the European Union. Would he be pleased to have 28? I don't know about Turkey, what he would say about Turkey. I think he would say we are condemned to succeed, to quote Edgard Pisani on the subject of other European negotiations. However, I think that he would be quite pleased that we had got so far from such small and modest beginnings. On one occasion - this is my last story - I was walking with him through the Berlaymont buildings in Brussels to go and have lunch with the Luxembourg Prime Minister, Jacques Santer. We were having a late lunch and all the functionaries were rushing back to their offices after having had a long lunch and I said, "Doesn't it seem funny to you to see all these people rushing around, this great big building and all this going on? It was once just a small piece of paper on your desk." He looked at it and said, "I know. It's horrible." Before the High Authority was established, he had said, "If we are more than two hundred and fifty we are lost." Personally he liked to work with small groups, but he realised that organising Europe was different.

Part Two

Federalist Campaigns, Political Parties and the Public since 1950

Britain's relations with the EC and the EU have been the long-standing, permanent political issues of the last half-century. Leading politicians and civil servants have understood the essentially federal nature of the integration process, whilst it has fallen to federalists to lead successful popular campaigns to ensure British participation in the Community and Union. Caught between the cross-currents of the political and economic advantages of wholehearted commitment and a wave of media campaigns to subvert any understanding of the true meanings of "federal" and "federalism", party attitudes have varied over time. At different times, albeit rarely simultaneously, all three major British political parties have supported an extension of European integration – the conferment of new competences on the joint institutions and increases in their decision-making capacity. Fear has played too large a part in determining British attitudes towards Europe – competing rival fears of being left outside a uniting Continent, fear that something undefined but unrecoverable will be lost through full participation.

Chapter 4

Campaigns for Accession to the EC and Against Withdrawal

Ernest Wistrich

FEDERALISTS HAVE LED FOUR PUBLIC CAMPAIGNS SUPPORTING BRITISH MEMBERSHIP OF THE EUROPEAN COMMUNITY: two in favour of accession and two against attempts to get Britain to withdraw from the Community. Two days after the Messina Conference in 1955 the Annual General Meeting of Federal Union urged full British participation in the Common Market as a first step to a European federation. Funds were raised, initially to finance a massive study, conducted by the Economist Intelligence Unit, on the effect on British industry of European free trade. The resulting publication in 1957 of a book entitled "Britain and Europe" sold more than 8,000 copies, raising funds well in excess of its original cost. These were used to establish a number of organisations: Britain in Europe, aimed at promoting European integration amongst industry, Europe House which held an impressive series of lectures, and the Common Market Campaign.

When the British Conservative Government announced its decision in 1961 to negotiate for membership of the European Community, public attitudes were highly favourable towards joining it. Nearly 50 per cent approved with less than 20 per cent against: the rest "did not know." The Common Market Campaign launched its work with a monthly broadsheet and several pamphlets. It set up regional committees in Glasgow and Manchester and employed three regional organisers to build support in selected parliamentary constituencies. The campaign continued until the French veto some 18 months later. Expenditure on that campaign - less than £10,000 - was very modest and well overshadowed by the much greater resources used by the Anti-Common Market League.

After exploratory negotiations conducted by the Labour Government in 1966-7 it was decided to make a second attempt to gain entry into the Community, a decision backed by an unprecedented 85 per cent vote in favour in the House of Commons in May 1967. Public enthusiasm for membership almost matched the views of their MPs. Seventy per cent were in favour with less than 10 per cent opposed. But at the end of November

1967 President de Gaulle issued his second veto. Public opinion changed dramatically as a result of this second rebuff. Nearly 50 per cent became opposed to membership, with those in favour dropping to about 35 per cent, and support continued to decline during the following years.

Federalists sought other ways to join. Back in 1966 they had set up a Campaign for a European Political Community. Following a series of studies conducted by the Federal Trust for Education and Research, a conference was held in Sussex in the summer of 1968 with the participation of delegates and observers from European Community countries. The object was to work out practical European policies in various fields not covered by the Rome Treaty. These included a technological community aimed at closing the growing technological gap between Europe and the US, the development of common economic policies providing effective aid to the third world and setting up a common European currency; and a common European foreign and defence policy. All these new policies were to form part of a new European Political Community, of which Britain, excluded from the EEC by de Gaulle, would be a founding member, and thus bypass the French veto against British participation in the further integration of Europe. The aim would be ultimately to merge the two European Communities into one.

The proposal was widely publicised by Britain in Europe both at home and on the Continent, receiving much support from fellow federalists in the European Community. George Brown, who had recently resigned as Foreign Secretary, decided to back the proposals. With Foreign Office support he travelled to EC capitals and persuaded most of the governments, apart from the French, to look favourably at the ideas advanced. Indeed the initiative led to a major diplomatic crisis between Britain and France. Having heard of George Brown's proposals, President de Gaulle invited the British Ambassador Sir Christopher Soames to whom he advanced a confidential counter-proposal for Britain to form part of a political directorate of the bigger European countries to control the EEC while retaining full national sovereignties. The British government, anxious not to be accused of double-dealing and supporting the proposals advanced by George Brown, decided to make public de Gaulle's suggestions and British rejection of them. This led to a diplomatic row and French suspension of normal diplomatic contacts with Britain and its Ambassador to France. In the meantime the public launch of the proposed European Political Community was planned to take place during the April 1969 London state visit of the Italian President Saragat. On the day on which the project was to be publicly launched jointly by the British and Italian governments, President de Gaulle resigned after losing a referendum on regional decentralisation in France. The planned Anglo-Italian proposal for a Political Community was transformed into a commitment to enlarge the EEC with a commitment to direct election of the European Parliament.

With the departure of President de Gaulle, his successor Georges Pompidou lifted the veto against UK membership and the Labour Government started to prepare for entry negotiations. To inform the public it published a White Paper early in 1970, setting out the estimated costs and benefits of membership. It carefully calculated the costs, particularly in relation to agriculture and food, but failed to estimate the benefits in concrete terms. This handed an additional weapon to the opponents of British membership.

In the meantime Britain in Europe decided to seek substantial backing for the expected campaign for entry. At a fund-raising dinner held at the Guildhall 800 guests listened to speeches by Prime Minister Harold Wilson, the Conservative leader Edward Heath and Liberal leader Jeremy Thorpe. As a result of their appeals some £450,00 was raised for Britain in Europe and its associated charity the European Educational Research Trust. At about the same time negotiations were conducted between Britain in Europe and the UK Council of the European Movement for a merger under the new name of the British Council of the European Movement. It was in effect a takeover of the European Movement, a declining organisation which tended to follow rather than lead government policy, by the expanding and predominantly federalist Britain in Europe.

When the Conservatives came to power in June 1970 the government took over the negotiating strategy prepared by the preceding Labour administration. It faced a dilemma. Negotiations promised to be complex and tough, especially in defence of British interests. Public opinion was generally hostile and by the end of the year only 18 per cent favoured entry with a massive 70 per cent against. Parliament was unlikely to approve entry against such a hostile public background. To meet the problem Geoffrey Rippon, the minister in charge of the negotiations, asked the newly merged European Movement to launch a campaign in favour of British entry.

The Movement accepted the challenge and raised further funds - mainly from business - to finance an intensive campaign. The first task was to set out solid and convincing arguments in favour and ensure their widest possible dissemination. Some 200 speakers were recruited and trained to address meetings throughout the country. Every conceivable organisation was encouraged to hold meetings for its members at which speakers from the European Movement explained the issues. During the first half of 1971 over 1,000 such meetings were held. Some involved debates with opponents but most consisted of our speakers setting out the reasons for and benefits of EEC membership, as well as the likely future developments of the Community in both economic and political terms.

Opponents of British membership have subsequently developed a myth that the arguments advanced at the time were merely for a free trade area. This was not the case: proposals for monetary and technological union and a Political Community with a directly elected European Parliament formed an important part of the arguments advanced by our speakers. A large number of leaflets were produced as was a monthly free newspaper called *The British European*. This was designed for a popular readership with cartoons and many photographs illustrating the benefits of EEC membership. Some ten million copies of leaflets and the newspaper were distributed freely by volunteers, who included girls wearing tee-shirts with the slogan "Europe or Bust." The campaign in the country was organised by paid regional organisers employed by the European Movement. A major advertising campaign was carried out in the national press over several months. Responding to claims that British entry would mean higher prices for butter, the European Movement launched a highly successful advert: a schoolboy and an associated text with the words "Give him cheap butter now and let him worry about where his bread is coming from later." Another advert – to counter the largely sceptical Labour movement - listed 100 Labour MPs strongly in favour of membership. Several hundred large wall posters were displayed on billboards showing children waving flags of EC and candidate countries over a slogan "Say YES to Europe." Articles and letters were prepared and organised to appear in the national, regional and local press, often written by prominent personalities with varied backgrounds and occupations. A pop record was produced of a song with the refrain "We've got to get in to get on." It was played at meetings and gained some popularity by being broadcast several times on radio. The same slogan was used on window bills and car stickers.

The campaign lasted some six months and cost around one million pounds. The funds were raised largely from business: none were provided by the government. By the end of the campaign, when negotiations for entry were concluded, public opinion had swung: there was a small majority in favour of membership. As a result parliamentarians, in approving the agreement reached, were not inhibited by the previous public hostility. In October 1971, by a majority of 112 votes, the House of Commons approved the negotiated terms of membership. The UK entered the EEC on 1st January 1973.

The Labour Party did not reject British membership of the Community, but objected to the terms negotiated by the Conservative Government. To avoid a split between pro- and anti-Europeans, the party made a commitment that, once returned to power, it would renegotiate the terms and, if successful, submit the results to a national referendum allowing party members freedom to campaign on either side of the argument. When Labour was returned to office in 1974 a referendum was clearly on the cards. This was to be the first national referendum in British constitutional history, without precedent or experience to guide its conduct.

Once again the European Movement started to plan for the forthcoming campaign. An in-depth survey of opinion was conducted in June 1974. The results showed a 2 to 1 majority against membership. The survey also set out to discover the reasons of those questioned for their attitudes and their reaction to various arguments advanced during the interview. The results helped to define the arguments to be put to the public in due course.

Because Britain lacked experience of referendums it was decided to investigate the conduct of the referendum campaigns on EEC membership held in 1972 in Ireland, Denmark and Norway. The first two countries obtained large majorities in favour of membership. In Norway the opposition won and the country did not join the Community. All these campaigns produced valuable data and techniques which could be applied in Britain. Particular attention was paid to the campaign in Norway especially that waged by the opponents of membership. There was almost unanimous support for entry from the establishment, consisting of the government, the largest political parties, business, trade unions and the media who all spoke with a single voice in favour of membership. In response the opposition developed a strategy which avoided the unanimity of the pro side. Opponents represented a wide variety of interests, each putting their own reasons for opposing EC membership. Thus Norwegian fishermen campaigned to preserve their territorial waters and traditional fishing rights. Protestants warned against the dangers posed by Rome and the dominant role of Catholics in the EC. Every town formed a local representative group of citizens who argued the disadvantages of EEC membership for their localities. The multiplicity of different arguments against overcame the solid and unanimous front of the establishment and those in favour of Norwegian entry were narrowly defeated in the referendum.

The European Movement decided to adopt a strategy similar to the Norwegian anti-EEC campaign, setting up many organisations, each campaigning independently with its own distinct views, though centrally co-ordinated. The Movement faced yet another dilemma. Its highly partisan campaign for entry in 1971 was felt by some to have been conducted by federalist eurofanatics: many otherwise favourably inclined non-governmental organisations might have expressed objections to working under the European Movement's umbrella. It was therefore decided to create, at the beginning of 1975 and for the duration of the referendum campaign, a new organisation, "Britain in Europe"; to suspend temporarily the activities of the Movement; and to transfer all its staff and supporters to the new body.

After the General Election in the autumn of 1974, which was won by Labour with a substantially increased majority, negotiations for changing the terms of membership were started. Legislation was introduced to hold the referendum after this was completed. The 6th of June 1975 was designated as the referendum date. In the legislation two official organisations were recognised as the respective protagonists of the YES and NO campaigns and each was allocated a government grant of £125,000. They were allowed to raise their own funds from private sources, but once the official campaign started, the names of all donors above £1,000 had to be declared.

Britain in Europe, leading the YES campaign, received endorsement from business, some trade unions, academics and from well-known politicians. The campaign was put into high gear at the beginning of 1975 and its slogan "Keep Britain in Europe" received the widest publicity.

To build up an active army of supporters the Movement had already in 1974 distributed some 6.5 million leaflets, reaching most households in the UK, entitled "Out of Europe - Out of Work" and appealing for volunteers to help with the forthcoming campaign. It yielded some 12,000 volunteers. Seventeen regional organisers were employed with the task of organising the helpers into appropriate groups and giving them guidance. Some 600 speakers were trained and they addressed several thousand meetings. Once again the arguments advanced included, not only the benefits of the Common Market, but also the aims of the Community to build a democratic and politically united Europe.

In every town, committees were formed such as "Brighton in Europe," "Oxford in Europe," etc. Each committee had a non-party chair, but included representatives of all the major political parties. Such co-operation was novel, but generally highly successful. Every local society and NGO favourably inclined was invited to take an active part. The local committee's principal role was to work out the reasons why their locality would benefit from membership of the EC and then to publicise them. Further supporters were recruited, leaflets, supplied from the centre, were distributed, meetings were organised, letters to editors and articles were placed in the local press, and participation in radio and TV programmes was encouraged. Apart from a small establishment grant of £30 from the centre, local committees were expected to raise their own funds. As the referendum date approached, 374 local groups had been set up and, under the guidance of regional organisers, they were active in preparing for and getting out the vote.

Every conceivable professional and cultural organisation was approached, encouraging their members to set up a group of supporters from their ranks. Such groups were formed for solicitors, doctors, authors, actors and other occupations and professions. Posters of well-known supporters from the worlds of art and sport were displayed. Newly set up organisations such as "Christians for Europe," "Women for Europe" and "Youth for Europe" were especially active. All these groups had the task of promoting the European cause amongst their peers from the point of view of their professional or sectoral interests. The main political parties campaigned independently, although they were centrally co-ordinated. Amongst smaller groupings "Communists for Europe" was set up in opposition to the official Communist Party which formed part of the NO campaign.

Shops were rented in prominent positions in several dozen urban centres to help distribute millions of leaflets, pamphlets, posters, campaign buttons, car stickers, window bills and other promotional materials. Large window displays attracted visitors and stocks of promotional material were freely handed out to all comers for wider distribution. Separate co-ordinating organisations were set up for Scotland, Wales and Northern Ireland. To counter widespread hostility to the EEC amongst the trade unions, several hundred industrial and trading enterprises were encouraged to study the effects of EEC membership on their businesses and then communicate the largely favourable results to their employees.

Mass public meetings were organised throughout the country with prominent politicians and other speakers from professional organisations and universities. Training was provided to assist speakers taking part in daily debates between pros and antis on radio and TV. A television film along the lines of a party political broadcast was shown on all channels alongside one produced by the NO campaign. Adverts were placed in both the national and regional press and large numbers of posters displayed on billboards throughout the country. During the last weekend before the referendum, through the encouragement of Christians for Europe, sermons and prayers were held in many churches appealing for a YES vote in the referendum. The whole campaign cost around £2 million and this excluded funds raised independently by the local and professional groups.

The National Referendum Campaign for the NO vote was led by a number of Labour cabinet ministers, who had the government's dispensation to work against its recommendation to approve the renegotiated terms. Among its supporters were politicians like Enoch Powell, Ian Paisley and Tony Benn as well as the majority of trade union leaders and several Conservative MPs, but it also included the neo-fascist National Front and the Communist Party. Although motivations for opposing membership were often quite divergent, they presented a unanimous front using the same arguments. Although some politicians raised the issue of loss of national sovereignty, the main thrust of the NO campaign concentrated on the rise in the cost of living, especially food. Particularly memorable was the visit made by Barbara Castle to the Continent to compare food prices with those in the UK: her comparative food basket received extensive media publicity. It may be that the general uniformity of views expressed lacked credibility and lost the NO campaigners support in the course of their campaign. Their financial resources were much smaller than those of the YES campaigners, largely because they had difficulties in finding support from business, most of which backed Britain in Europe. They spent about £250,000 including the £125,000 government grant given to each side. 64.5 per cent of the electorate took part in the referendum held on 6 June 1975, of whom 67 per cent voted YES and 33 per cent NO.

The second attempt to get Britain out of the Community came as a result of the decision of the Labour Party Conference in 1980, held a year after losing the General Election to Mrs. Thatcher. The party voted massively for unconditional withdrawal from the EEC without a further referendum, if elected to govern at the next General Election. One consequence was to stimulate the creation of the Social Democratic Party to which the majority of Labour European federalists moved.

By the end of 1982, as the General Election approached, a majority of the public had once again swung against membership. The European Movement decided to launch and base its campaign on recently published research which estimated that some 2.5 million jobs in the UK were dependent on continued membership of the EC. This was publicised throughout the country, especially amongst trade unionists. Once again the Movement's campaign helped to swing public opinion. According to polls conducted at the June 1983 General Election there was a 2 to 1 majority in favour of staying in the Community. This probably contributed to Labour's heavy defeat, with the Social Democratic Party almost overtaking Labour. Following the election Labour gradually distanced itself from a policy of withdrawal and moved towards supporting membership and further European integration.

Although not large in numbers, federalists played a leading role in getting the UK to join the Community and preventing subsequent attempts at withdrawal. They also provided support and continued to campaign for further integration aimed, ultimately, at the creation of a federal United States of Europe.

Bibliography

David Butler and Uwe Kitzinger, *The 1975 Referendum* (Basingstoke: Macmillan, 1976, 2nd edn 1996).

Uwe Kitzinger, *Diplomacy and Persuasion - How Britain joined the Common Market* (London: Thames & Hudson, 1973).

Richard Mayne and John Pinder, *Federal Union: The Pioneers* (Basingstoke: Macmillan, 1990).

David Spanier, *Europe our Europe: The Inside Story of the Common Market Negotiations* (London: Martin Secker & Warburg, 1972).

Ernest Wistrich, 'The Lessons of the 1975 Referendum', in Roger Beetham (ed.), *The Euro Debate* (London: Federal Trust, 2002).

Chapter 5

British Political Parties and the Dreaded 'f' Word

Richard Corbett MEP

WHEN I WAS ASKED TO SPEAK AT THE MADISON TRUST CONFERENCE, my first reaction was, "Oh yes, fine." When I was later told the subject, I said "Hang on a minute, half the room will know more about this than I do!" I was told not to worry, just to introduce a discussion and not go through the whole history of all of Britain's political parties and their relationship to Europe. So, no exhaustive history, rather my focus will be on broad trends and contradictions.

The press must take much of the blame for the fact that the word "federal" or "federalist" is equated, in Britain, with the idea of a centralised "superstate" rather than what we in this room know federalism to really be about. Their consistent and repetitive use of the term "federal superstate" is one of the reasons why, in all political parties now, the term "federal Europe" tends to be avoided - at least as an object of desirable policy (rather as something that parties want to campaign *against*!). Advocating a federal Europe as a good thing has become taboo in Britain.

Even pro-European organisations shy away from the term. The European Movement used to display its affiliation to the Union of European Federalists on its membership cards – no longer. The Young European Federalists that I belonged to when I was a student is now the Young European Movement. The new pro-European business organisation – Business for a New Europe – actually has in its statement of principles that they are pro-Europe but "against old-fashioned federalism." Whatever old-fashioned federalism is supposed to be, they are against it - and that is in a pro-European statement from a pro-European body! In the European Parliament, there is an all party Federalist Intergroup for a European Constitution, but I think only two British MEPs have ever attended.

Of course this situation is not entirely the fault of the media. Britain is peculiar in that in no other member state is there such a highly organised and well-financed anti-Europe campaign - in fact many campaigns, because if you look even briefly over the web you will find at least a dozen anti-European campaigning organisations that are out there day and night, organising people to write letters to editors of even local newspapers across the country, that are there with their soundbites, that are there with their publications, and so on, non-stop.

That has played a major role in stimulating what we now (inaccurately) call "euroscepticism." It has also resulted in the reappearance of a factor relevant to the 1975 referendum – namely, triangulation. Moderate pro-Europeans and governments tend to go for a facile middle ground in the debate on Europe: "of course we are not for withdrawal, that would be silly, nor are we in favour of a superstate - of course not, we are taking the reasonable middle ground."

Sometimes, however, the vocabulary of pro-Europeans saying they are against a "centralised superstate" slips to being against a "federal superstate," and then against anything federal. For a long time Labour was very careful to stick to opposing a "centralised" superstate, but in recent months I've noticed, not just from the government but elsewhere, that nuance has disappeared, which makes it even more difficult for those of us who do want to get some coherent idea of what federalism really means across to people.

It was not ever thus. Until some years ago some of our parties at least had lively internal debates on federalism. The Liberals for many years supported the federal objective openly and explicitly. They were the most consistent of all our parties in terms of their commitment to Europe in general, and even with a vision of what that meant in its long-term development. They didn't shy away from using the word "federalism." They still use it sometimes in relation to internal possibilities within the UK, but no longer in relation to Europe. Michael Steed explained to me that Liberals are intellectually predisposed to federalism as if they were sort of genetically preprogrammed towards it. But nonetheless in recent years the Liberal Party – Liberal Democrats now - do not use the term as an objective of their European policy.

Labour of course was never explicitly committed as a party to federalism in the European context, or indeed in any other context as far as I know, except perhaps long ago in the mists of time. But it was at least used approvingly by some people in the debate within the party – you don't necessarily need to go back to the 1940s but it is worth remembering that famous motion signed by 100 Labour MPs "to affirm Britain's readiness to federate with any other nation willing to do so on the basis of a federal constitution to be agreed by a representative assembly." This was tabled as a motion in 1947 and again in almost identical terms in 1948. When Denis Healey argued against federalism with his paper *Feet on the Ground* Labour federalists responded - "you mean Heads in the Sand." In other words, there was an actual debate on federalism: its merits and demerits.

It continued in the 1950s and '60s. Gaitskell's famous speech from 1962 rejecting membership of the European Community is interesting. If you read the full text, rather than the bit that's most often quoted, his argument was that the Community was inevitably going to develop into a federation – it was quite logical for it to do so; but for this very reason Britain, as the centre of the Commonwealth, could not participate in it. So he accepted the federal logic, accepted that it would and indeed should develop into a federal-type system but that was his argument for Britain not to be part of it because of the Commonwealth – a curiously old-fashioned view for a socialist!

During the Labour Party's splits in the '70s and '80s the term federalism disappeared even in internal debate within the party. The pro-Europeans were not going to stick their necks out even further - they were trying already then, I suppose, to triangulate. But once the party came back to a pro-European position in the late '80s, early '90s then you did see the term appearing from time to time. Labour MEPs explicitly voted in a meeting of the European Parliamentary Labour Party (EPLP) that they supported a union of federal type – this was in the context of the then Maastricht negotiations. The TUC, with other trade unions in Europe in the ETUC, were willing to say that their objective "is a federation of democratic and social European States." The Labour Movement for Europe right up to the year 2002 published pamphlets arguing that the word federalism has been systematically misunderstood in Britain and what we have now is actually already a union of federal type and we ought to get used to it and try to reappropriate the word for normal political discourse.

So until relatively recently there was a revival in discussions in the Labour Party using the term, at least by some people, but this has now disappeared. Members have just given up trying it because in the public mind it is so associated with centralised superstate and everything that nobody wants. I did try to insert it when asked to contribute to one of the Prime Minister's speeches on Europe. I put in a whole bit along the lines of saying that federalism is a question of definition: if you mean centralised superstate well there's actually nobody who supports it or hardly anybody across Europe. If you mean different levels of government responsible for different matters, as decentralised as possible but centralised where necessary, and with democratic accountability at each level, isn't that what we have now in the European Union, more or less? I think that very quickly had a red line through it when it went through the machinery at No 10. Gordon Brown's views on these things do not persuade me that he is going to lead the way in reviving use of the term.

Then there is the Conservative Party. Similarly it was never an explicit objective of the Conservative Party to build a federal Europe but, until recently, it too had members willing to use the term and actually call themselves federalists such as Sir Anthony Meyer in the House of Commons. Some past leaders of their MEP delegation, Tom Spencer, Christopher Prout (now Lord Kingsland), Bill Newton-Dunn – who has since left the Conservative Party – were until a few years ago willing explicitly to say they were federalists. Sir Christopher Prout said: "Federalism involves the transfer of power by States to a common authority. Each time the Council adopts a regulation its terms become legally binding on member states so day by day we're building up a federal system." I cannot envisage any of their current MEPs being willing to say that now. The pro-European Tories are falling by the wayside, often leaving the party on that very issue: Bill Newton-Dunn, Hugh Dykes, Robert Jackson, Emma Nicholson, Peter Price, Peter Temple-Morris, Brendan Donnelly, to name but a few.

Perhaps it came to a crunch in the Maastricht negotiations where early drafts replaced the words "ever closer union" with reference to a union of federal type or to a federal objective. Interestingly, that sat on the negotiation table for several weeks without British Conservative ministers objecting to it, until the press got hold of the story in Britain and immediately there was an objection that this wording was unacceptable. As we know, it was eventually taken out at the Maastricht summit itself - left to the end to enable John Major to claim a victory over federalism at the end of the negotiations.

It is interesting that there is currently an intense debate within the Conservative Party about leaving the group of the European Peoples Party (EPP) in the European Parliament on the ground that the EPP Group is explicitly federalist in its outlook. I just point out there are other non-federalists in the EPP – Ulster Unionists, Czech ODS, the French Gaullists and various Scandinavian Conservatives. The EPP is indeed far wider, but the cited reason for departure is that the group is explicitly federalist. So obsessed with opposing federalism have the Conservatives become, that they would rather sit in impotent isolation or with unsavoury extremist parties than be part of a broad coalition that includes federalists!

So much for attitudes to the word "federal"! The paradox is that, despite this, the parties have supported incremental steps along the road to federalism. I subscribe to the view most eloquently expressed by John Pinder, that the process of integration involves incremental steps towards a federal system and that we now have a system which incorporates a number of federal characteristics. Perhaps, like Molière's *Bourgeois Gentilhomme* who never realised he was speaking prose all his life, so it is with federalism and the European Union: we are in a strange but functioning federal-type system, with some lacunae and unusual features, but nonetheless a union of federal type. Let me draw attention to five specific (there are actually more) areas of Community activity. At one time or another all three main parties have been in favour of, and even supported, the strengthening of these features.

The first way in which the Union is more than just a typical international organisation is that its scope is so wide: a common market (with common rules for that market on competition, state aids, consumer protection, workers' rights, aspects of social policy, health and safety rules, environmental standards and much else); a single currency; several common policies including the ambition of a common foreign and security policy; exclusive competence for external trade, and so on. Second, European law has primacy over national law and is enforced by a common Supreme Court and legal system. Third, its executive body, albeit not a very strong one, is independent of national governments once it's been nominated. Its members cannot be recalled by those national governments; but it is accountable to the European Parliament. Fourth, the Council, the body that represents the states, votes in most cases by majority – or more precisely by a qualified majority – and not by unanimity. Fifth, it has an elected European Parliament with designated powers. All these typical federal features ensure that the European Union stands apart from traditional international organisations.

Now every single one of these federal features has been expanded over the last few years and each time it was with the approval of at least two out of three of the main British political parties and sometimes all three of them. Over a 20-year period there were four IGCs that led to treaty revisions requiring national ratification: the Single European Act, the Maastricht Treaty, the Amsterdam Treaty and the Nice Treaty. Each one did only a few things, but cumulatively they have transformed the European Community as it was in the early '80s to a quite different European Union at the beginning of this new century or millennium. The Constitutional Treaty would have taken that a step further but I'll leave that out of the debate for the time being.

Let me enlarge on these five points from an institutional perspective. The scope of the Union – its field of competence - was increased by the Single European Act not just to beef up the commitment to a common (single) market by setting a deadline of 1992 and giving more means to achieve it, but adding new chapters to the Treaty with new competences explicitly empowering the Union to act on environment, on research and development and bringing in for the first time a codification of political co-operation in foreign policy. The Maastricht Treaty then took that further by including monetary union as a part of the Union's field of activities – a single currency in due course, operated by a federal Central Bank. It also added to the treaties new chapters on transeuropean networks, development policy, education, public health, culture, and consumer protection; it strengthened the previous provisions on regional policy; it upgraded and strengthened political co-operation into a common foreign and security policy (admittedly in a separate, largely – though not entirely - intergovernmental "pillar") and for the first time provided for co-operation on justice and home affairs in another largely intergovernmental "third pillar." Six years later, the Amsterdam Treaty went a bit further on the scope of European Union powers, in that it transferred part of the third pillar into the Community pillar and gave the Union powers to adopt non-discrimination legislation. Four years later, the Treaty of Nice beefed up the references to defence and security co-operation, and set up EUROJUST to start co-operation between prosecuting authorities. So each of these treaties has reinforced the scope of the Union's competences.

My second federalist feature was European law, enforced by a common court. Well, of course that was there from the beginning but the Single European Act strengthened the capacity of the legal system of the Union to actually work by providing for a Court of First Instance. Given that the Court of Justice was becoming gridlocked by the number and backlog of cases, this enormously increased the capacity of the European legal system. In the Maastricht Treaty there were further transfers of power to the Court of First Instance so as to increase its capacity. Maastricht also gave the Court of Justice the power to fine member states. Finally, the Nice Treaty allowed both courts much more leeway to meet in chambers rather than the full court and provided for subsidiary specialised courts to be set up. So, incrementally - treaty by treaty - the capacity of the legal system of the Union has been increased. This is fundamental: the rule of law is the basis for the Union.

Regarding the third issue I mentioned the Commission as an executive: a political executive with a degree of autonomy from the member states. The Single European Act didn't do much, but it did make it clear that implementing powers should normally be conferred upon the Commission (subject to the "comitology" system) rather than the Council reserving implementing powers to itself. The latter is now very much the exception. The Maastricht Treaty brought in more political changes. It changed the term of office of the Commission from four to five years to follow the cycle of European parliamentary elections, and laid down that each new Parliament has to confirm a new Commission for the latter to take office. As Parliament was already able to dismiss a Commission with a vote of no confidence, this made it much more explicit that the Commission needed to have the confidence of Parliament. This has since been demonstrated by the fall of the Santer Commission and the need for Barroso to change and reshuffle his Commission to obtain a vote of confidence. The Amsterdam Treaty gave Parliament the right to approve or reject (Parliament's Rules of Procedure say "elect," as does the constitutional treaty) the President designate of the Commission. The Nice Treaty gave the Commission President the power to reshuffle the college of Commissioners, to appoint Vice Presidents and dismiss individual Commissioners. It also made the choice by the European Council of a President designate of the Commission a subject for qualified majority rather than unanimous vote.

The resultant system implies that Council has to nominate as President somebody capable of gaining a Parliamentary majority. The concept began to take hold last time when the EPP, which was the largest group after the European elections, said they would not accept a socialist President of the Commission and the European Council did not consider any socialists for that job (even though Vitorino would perhaps have been a far better choice). Whilst the Council did not formally acknowledge the link, the debate certainly took account of the political position in the European Parliament. It remains to be seen whether this will be taken still further, with the main European political parties nominating candidates for President ahead of the European parliamentary elections (as the Greens did last time). In any event, as a result of these four treaties, the nature of the Commission as a political executive has been enhanced, step by step.

With regard to qualified majority voting, this was extended by all of the four treaties. In each case the extensions were limited, but cumulatively it's been an enormous turnaround. It is worth bearing in mind that before the Single European Act, there were in practice very few formal votes in the Council.

Finally, there is the fifth item - the elected Parliament and its powers. The Single European Act introduced the so-called co-operation procedure (where Parliament was given a second reading but power remained with Council) and the Assent Procedure (with Parliamentary approval necessary for Association agreements or Accession treaties). The big breakthrough was the Maastricht Treaty which introduced the codecision procedure with Parliament's approval (as well as that of the Council) needed to enact European legislation. In effect this was the birth of a bicameral legislative authority, consisting of the directly elected Parliament and the Council – the latter in effect a Chamber of States. There would be up to three readings in each body to consider legislation. Under Maastricht, this actually only applied to ten articles in the treaty. The Amsterdam Treaty took that further and also changed the procedure to Parliament's advantage. The Nice Treaty added still more areas to codecision, so that the bulk of European Union legislation is now subject to it or to the widened assent procedure. Not only is this more democratic; a two-chamber legislature is certainly more federal in nature.

Maastricht also gave Parliament the right to vote on the Commission; to elect an Ombudsman; the power to establish Committees of Inquiry; limited rights to initiate legislative proposals; and the ability to access the court. Initially this latter only applied when Parliament was defending its own prerogatives - a limitation deleted by the Nice Treaty. Finally Maastricht recognised the right of citizens to petition the European Parliament. So here we have a series of measures to ensure that the European Parliament is an effective player on the political scene. What could have been characterised as little more than a talking shop previously, and with few powers, was now actually given some real teeth.

Incrementally, then, all these features, these five federal characteristics, have been reinforced over time.

Now, back to the political parties. In all cases these steps were supported by two of our three main political parties in Britain. The Liberal Democrats have, of course, been consistent - they supported these measures through-out. The positions of Conservative and Labour are both more complex and perhaps more interesting – because they have been in government and able to deliver. The two parties have also undergone a contradictory evolution.

The Single European Act was supported and enacted by a Conservative Government who were willing to swallow what had been signed after negotiations in Brussels and Luxembourg and put it through the House of Commons. Labour opposed it. This was at the time when Labour was beginning to rethink its position on Europe, had retreated from a "withdrawalist" position but was not yet ready to endorse a position of going forward. It didn't oppose the Single European Act very vigorously but it still opposed it.

The Maastricht Treaty was, of course, officially supported by both Labour and the Conservatives as well as the Liberals - but with some complexities. The first time the Maastricht bill came before the House of Commons, it sailed through its first major reading by a very large majority with very little controversy. But after the Danish first referendum on Maastricht, John Major suspended consideration of the bill at committee stage and only came back to it nearly a year later - by which time the eurosceptic wing of his party had organised. Although a minority, this group did not hesitate to oppose the bill at every turn, even to the extent of imperilling the government's survival. This ensured that the process of ratification was highly contentious and very damaging for the Conservative Party. Although the bill did get through in the end, it left a legacy of bitter division within the Conservatives and a great strengthening of their eurosceptic wing, who got their teeth into this battle, gained focus and finance. The debate allowed many a young radical Tory to make a name as a vigorous eurosceptic, with guaranteed press coverage.

Labour's position was to support the ratification of the treaty but to make life difficult for the government. It was too good an opportunity to miss, given the nature of British adversarial politics. However, Labour also wanted more. The Conservatives had opted out of the Social Chapter. Labour said Britain should ratify this treaty with the Social Chapter. This could not simply be achieved by amending the bill, as the opt-out was in the treaty that was signed, so any amendments to that effect were ruled out of order. One new MP, who was still simultaneously an MEP at that time – Geoff Hoon – won the Parliamentarian of the Year Award from The Guardian for coming up with an amendment which said that the government would deposit the instrument of ratification of this treaty once it has notified its partners in the European Union that it intends to sign up to the Social Chapter – an amendment which, because it did not change the treaty, was allowable. This was supported by Labour, the Liberal Democrats, the SNP and Plaid Cymru. They were joined opportunistically by some Tory rebels, for whom the Social Chapter was anathema, but who saw the opportunity to thwart the government. It resulted in a dead-heat vote in the Commons on the amendment. After chaotic scenes, the treaty was eventually approved with Britain's opt-out intact.

That is the only treaty in the entire history of European integration where the official position of all three major British parties was in favour. However, that remarkable fact did not usher in a new era of consensus on Europe. Rather, it went unnoticed in the complexities surrounding the ratification debate with the divisions between parties over the Social Chapter and the divisions within the Conservatives over the whole treaty.

When it came to the Amsterdam Treaty, the two ships had simply and completely crossed in the night. Labour supported the treaty whilst the Conservatives were against it. But perhaps more interesting here is the fact that Labour took over the negotiations on that treaty in the very last months of the IGC and actually completely reversed the British negotiating position on some issues which were of great significance to anyone interested in the federal development of the European Union. The Conservative Government had opposed any extension of qualified majority voting. It had opposed both the extension of the scope of the codecision procedure and the changes mooted to it in favour of the European Parliament; it still opposed signing up to the Social Chapter; it opposed the proposal that had originated with the Swedish government for a new employment chapter of the treaty; it opposed any transfers from the Third Pillar on foreign and security policy to the Community Pillar and it even had advocated giving Council the right to overturn judgments of the Court of Justice. Now, on every single one of those points Labour reversed the British position when it came to power right towards the end of the IGC. Without that change of government, the Amsterdam Treaty would not have contained anything useful. There might not even have been an Amsterdam Treaty or if there were one it would have been very minimal indeed. That was a crossing point where the Conservatives had become what Labour had been 15 or 20 years previously – the party that opposed the development of the Union.

Labour knew what it was doing. Its positions on these issues had been carefully prepared in a working group of the four most senior shadow ministers and leading MEPs. The broad lines had even been approved by the previous party conference. In the IGC, prior to the election, a Labour official (RC) attended to assist the European Parliament representative, Elisabeth Guigou, ensuring that the Labour leadership had full information and documentation in preparation for taking over as the government.

The Nice Treaty was less spectacular, of course, in that it didn't contain so much, but it certainly confirmed the trend of the Conservatives to an outright hostile position and the trend in the hyperbole of the discourse and the debate about it. Labour and the Liberals supported the Nice Treaty.

So all this shows that, despite their rhetoric of ignoring or being against federalism, specific steps that reinforced the federal character of the Union have been supported by our governments of whatever colour and by our political parties: consistently by the Liberal Democrats, inconsistently by the others. Is it possible that this could still be the case in the future? Much depends upon what will happen next and when it will happen. Will the Constitutional Treaty or parts of it be salvaged in one way or another? The Liberal Democrats and Labour were, of course, for the Constitutional Treaty (Labour's manifesto referred to campaigning "wholeheartedly" for it), despite a context that is still more difficult than before in terms of domestic political debate. To be noted in this context are the rise of UKIP in the European elections; the press being perhaps even more against; the Conservatives, as the main opposition party, being now pretty united and resolute against the treaty and almost everything it contains. Indeed, since the French referendum, some trade unions and even some prominent figures in the Labour Party have come out against attempts to salvage it.

So, in terms of further steps forward, there is no guarantee that any radical steps will be supported. If there does have to be a referendum, given what happened in France and the Netherlands, the prospect of supporting more incremental steps in a federal direction are probably more limited than they have been in the last few years. Not impossible I would argue – I would hope – but certainly more difficult.

As to the use of the f-word, it will be a tall order. Can we make the word "federal" respectable once again? Even as a federalist I rarely use the word myself except in informed circles or unless I actually have the time to explain it to a captive audience. Of course the James Madison Trust is doing a wonderful job in stimulating debate and interest in academic circles. Federal Union makes a brave attempt, but there is such a tide in this respect that I have to say I remain very pessimistic. I suspect we need a more populist campaign group willing to write letters to editors of newspapers, place articles here and there, challenge misuse of the word in the media, etc. That might be the only way in which you could begin to turn around the reluctance to use the word in its proper sense in Britain. This is perhaps the real challenge that faces federalists in Britain.

Chapter 6

Time to Stop Being Afraid of Europe?

Brendan Donnelly

Editor's note

Towards the end of this article, its writer mentions the possibility of agreement on a "reduced version" of the European Constitutional Treaty, a possibility which essentially came to pass with the Lisbon Treaty of December, 2007. In describing this Treaty, the British government has laid great stress upon the "opt-outs" and "red lines,' which supposedly differentiate the United Kingdom's accession to the Treaty from that of others. Such defensive and self-centred rhetoric suggests that the underlying analysis of this article, written when the Treaty was only a gleam in Mr. Sarkozy's eye, is no less valid in 2008 than it was in 2006. There remain in the United Kingdom considerable ambiguities and uncertainties in both popular and political attitudes towards the European Union. These ambiguities represent an obvious check upon the otherwise natural evolution of the Union. They also represent an equally obvious diminution of the United Kingdom's capacity to define a coherent and sustainable view of its own position in the world. It is also yet another lost opportunity to promote at popular level a deeper understanding of the real nature of the European Union.

OVER THE PAST 50 YEARS, A NUMBER OF DIFFERING, SOMETIMES CONTRADICTORY, FEARS have shaped the approach of successive British governments to the European Community and the European Union. Fear of exclusion from important decision-making fora of their closest neighbours has always been a powerful restraining factor for Prime Ministers and Foreign Secretaries inclined to stand aside from new policies or institutions of European integration. At the same time the desire to be part of the European mainstream has never entirely eradicated an insular fear in Britain's leaders of irrevocable commitment to ever-closer political integration with continental Europe. The history of Britain's relationship with the European Community and Union has been largely a chronicle of these two fears and of which was the predominant emotion in any particular epoch. The period at which this article is written (autumn

2006) is arguably a time in which, unusually, neither of these traditional fears looms large in the British collective consciousness. But it is difficult to believe that these twin demons have been exorcised entirely from British attitudes towards the European Union. Forthcoming events, notably the revival of discussion about the stalled European Constitutional Treaty, may reanimate one or more probably both of these twin British apprehensions about the course of European integration.

It is a familiar observation that, throughout most of its national history, British European policy has been shaped by the desire to prevent any single power from gaining predominance in continental Europe. At the beginning of the nineteenth century this single power might have been France, and at the century's end it seemed to be Germany. Fear of German hegemony in Europe was the single most powerful factor persuading reluctant British governments to involve the British Empire in the First and Second World Wars. The defeat and partition of Germany in 1945 resolved for the foreseeable future one European threat from the horizon of British policy-makers, but confronted the United Kingdom with another, that of the Soviet Union. In response to this new threat, the United Kingdom was among the most enthusiastic advocates of, and contributors to, an innovative military alliance, the North Atlantic Treaty Organisation (NATO). This alliance involved an unprecedented and continuing degree of military integration among its signatories. British willingness to countenance this high degree of sovereignty sharing was initially buttressed by widespread genuine and justifiable fear among all sections of British society in face of potential Soviet aggression. When the Soviet military threat disappeared in the 1980s, the British government of the day and its successors came to see the justification for the alliance's continuation in the fear that without it the United States might lose its interest in Europe. Since the Second World War, British foreign policy has taken it as axiomatic that a strong American presence in Europe was in Europe's interest generally and in Britain's national interest specifically. Britain's reluctance to share its political sovereignty with its European neighbours has rarely been mirrored by similar hesitations about sharing its military sovereignty with the distant superpower, the United States.

Whereas in the 1950s the Soviet Union was a sufficiently powerful and imminent threat from the European Continent to command British attention, the founding of what is now the European Union in 1957 aroused no such interest. Few commentators in the United Kingdom thought it likely that the Treaty of Rome would change significantly the political structures of Western Europe, and Britain's relative post-war economic decline had not yet become the national obsession that it was in the late 1960s and 1970s. Robust defiance of the hegemonic aspirations of the Soviet Union in the 1950s was entirely consonant with well-established British attitudes to continental Europe. The Treaty of Rome, with its clear aspiration to redefine intra-European relations through an "ever-closer" union among the peoples of Europe, confronted British policy-makers in the 1950s with questions which they, as yet, could see no interest in considering, let alone answering.

The 15 years between the signing of the Treaty of Rome and British accession to the Treaty in 1972 saw a steady erosion in such dismissive and uninterested British attitudes towards the emerging "Common Market." It became apparent that the six original signatories of the Treaty of Rome had created a permanent new feature of Western Europe's political landscape, a numerically and economically powerful coalition which, if assembled in the eighteenth or nineteenth century, would have provoked anxious British attempts either to destroy it or to create an alternative, counterbalancing political constellation. In the 1960s, however, successive British governments came to realise that neither of these options was open to them. The Common Market was not going to disappear and the British-inspired European Free Trade Association had little plausibility as an alternative to what the Six had created. Under peaceful democratic conditions, Britain's European neighbours had succeeded in establishing what monarchies and dictatorships had failed to achieve militarily - the construction of a European coalition too powerful for the British to ignore and too cohesive to be undermined externally. The painfulness of this dilemma was only accentuated throughout the 1960s, when the general economic performance of France, Germany, Italy and the Benelux countries was noticeably superior to that of the United Kingdom. British fears of both political isolation and accelerating economic backwardness were at the root of two unsuccessful attempts by the United Kingdom to join the European Community before Edward Heath's successful application in the early 1970s. These fears were at their height in 1975, when the Prime Minister of the day, Harold Wilson, attempted to heal divisions within his own Labour Party about British membership of the European Community by holding a referendum on the subject. By a substantial majority the British electorate opted to remain within the Community, thereby conforming to the overwhelming tendency of constitutional referendums globally to endorse the status quo. As Winston

Churchill's son-in-law, Christopher Soames, graphically expressed it, 1975 was "not the time for Britain to leave a Christmas club, let alone the Common Market."

If the result of the referendum of 1975 was proof positive that at that date the British feared being outside the European Community more than they feared being inside it, the British debate surrounding accession itself in 1973 and the following referendum also reflected the other, contradictory, British fear about their position in Europe - that of being subsumed in an overarching European political entity of which the Treaty of Rome was simply a precursor. Some at least of those who in 1975 voted for Britain to remain in the European Union did so on the basis of predictions and reassurances from British politicians about the future course and nature of European integration. These were probably sincere, but were sometimes partial and over-simplified. The central goal of the Treaty of Rome - an ever-closer union among its signatories - is not merely a rhetorical or symbolic one, but a definite goal underpinned by a system of central European institutions, with autonomous rights and competences. In their eagerness to contradict absurd and over-drawn claims by some of its critics that the Treaty of Rome is a recipe for the destruction of the British state, some of its advocates in Britain in the 1970s and since have in their turn taken the easy and apparently rhetorically effective path of understating the fundamentally integrative workings and structure of the Treaty of Rome.

In the short term, this rhetorical evasion has been reassuring for British voters. In the longer term, it has set up a dangerous disjunction between the British debate on the future of the European Union and that occurring in most other member states of the Union. British electors have been led all too often by their political leaders to believe that for its future development the European Union must make a Manichean choice between the preferred British model of co-operation, collaboration and intergovernmentalism and the alleged federalist continental model of a European superstate. Since it is clear that the Treaty of Rome does not and cannot correspond to the first of those models, it has become fatally easy for the Treaty's opponents in Britain to argue that the second is an accurate characterisation of the Treaty and what follows from it. The failure of British politicians and opinion-formers to develop a rhetoric and analysis of European institutional integration - one which would be both accurate and reassuring for the electorate - is understandable. The adversarial nature of British politics has always encouraged the main party of opposition to play upon the largely irrational fears of the British electorate about the supposedly all-pervasive nature of the emergent so-called European superstate. British governments of both main political colours have frequently concluded that it was too difficult to mount a radical challenge to these fears: it was simpler to accept the existence of the fears and claim that the government of the day was no less robust than the Opposition in protecting the British public against those in continental Europe who wanted to call into being what the British electorate rightly feared and rejected. This equivocation has been a recurrent feature of British political discourse about European integration and Britain's role within it.

Even if the debate of the early 1970s only imperfectly quelled one set of British concerns relating to European integration, fear of isolation within the European Community remained for most of Margaret Thatcher's premiership in the 1980s a powerful component of British attitudes towards Europe. She reluctantly accepted the calling of the Intergovernmental Conference which led to the Single European Act when she realised in 1985 that all the other 11 member states were firmly ranged against her. In her celebrated Bruges speech of 1988, Margaret Thatcher articulated in striking terms her fear and that of a number of British voters that the United Kingdom would lose its political freedom of action within a "European superstate." Her speech was the beginning of a process whereby the Conservative Party, for many years primarily actuated by the fear of British isolation in Europe, became the populist articulator of the fear that Britain would be destroyed by Europe. Although this fear was one which continued and continues to lurk within the subconscious mind of many British voters, it is ironically the Conservative Party which has been led to the brink of destruction by its obsession over the past decade and a half with the stoking of mean-minded and exaggerated apprehensions on European issues in the British electorate.

This destructive process took time for its fulfilment. The apprehension that her policies on the exchange rate mechanism and the single European currency were driving the United Kingdom irrevocably to the margin of European decision-making was the immediate cause of Mrs. Thatcher's deposition as Prime Minister in 1990. No Conservative candidate who sought to succeed her in that year claimed to share her apocalyptic vision of the European Community. Her successor, John Major, knew that the prospect of British isolation within the European Union was worrying to many voters. He attempted publicly to distance himself from Thatcher's

European policies by insisting that he wanted to see Britain "at the heart of Europe."

Unfortunately, John Major's initial European rhetoric and his subsequent erratic European policy bore little relationship to each other. The arrangement he negotiated at Maastricht for Britain to postpone indefinitely its decision on whether to join the single European currency was an incomparable example of the paralysis in British European policy caused by contradictory fears of both participation in and isolation from the process of European integration. The Prime Minister's domestic weakness made him increasingly vulnerable to eurosceptic pressure from within his own Conservative Party, pressure which his opponents in the Labour Party gleefully exploited. Britain's bitter isolation from its European neighbours over the contentious issue of BSE was a sad but fitting end to the uncertain European diplomacy of John Major. His time as Prime Minister bequeathed to British public opinion a new fear to complement existing concerns, namely that Britain would always be within the European Union a victim of hostile coalitions ranged against it. Tony Blair came to power in 1997 promising, as John Major had, to make a better job of European policy than had his predecessor.

Blair's version of Major's aspiration for Britain to be "at the heart of Europe" was that he would "never allow Britain to be isolated in Europe." In pursuit of this goal, Tony Blair signed the Amsterdam Treaty in 1997 and the Nice Treaty in 2000, both being treaties rejected by the Conservative Opposition. For a number of years, both Blair's supporters and opponents believed he was preparing the ground for a referendum on British membership of the single European currency. In reality, his preparations for this possible referendum were little more than a vague confidence in his own ability as a political campaigner when propitious circumstances presented themselves. For New Labour, European issues were always seen as an instrument to embarrass the Conservative Party rather than as an expression of any deeply-held strategic view of Britain's position in the world. Insofar as he had a more detailed strategy, Blair seems to have believed that he could in a referendum on the single European currency exploit traditional British fears about economic and political isolation in Europe. At the same time he would reassure British voters fearful of continuing European political integration that the question of joining the single currency was a largely technical and economic matter, with only limited constitutional implications. It must be more than doubtful whether the intrinsic tension within this strategy could have survived the relentless scrutiny of a referendum campaign. Like all British political parties, New Labour is forced in general elections to appeal to different and disparate political audiences, a technique it has deployed with much success. It would, however, have been extremely difficult to run a referendum campaign on the single issue of the euro in such a fashion.

What is certain, however, is that Britain is today psychologically a great deal further away from joining the single European currency than it was when Tony Blair became Prime Minister. Many of those who believed that under his premiership Britain would join the single European currency expected that the United Kingdom would suffer demonstrable economic harm through standing aside from the euro. This sometimes put them in the politically unenviable position of appearing to hope that the United Kingdom would lose some of the economic ground it has made up in recent years on its European neighbours. Others hoped that the eurozone would exert so powerful an attractive force on the United Kingdom, both politically and economically, that rapid British membership would become inevitable. The City of London was sometimes envisaged as a leading advocate of British membership of the single currency, on the supposed ground that its currency-related operations would suffer from sterling's exclusion from the eurozone.

None of these expectations have come to pass. Britain's economic performance outside the eurozone has been relatively good; indeed in recent years it has been noticeably better than that of some other large countries within the single currency area. The City of London has not suffered, and indeed seems unlikely to suffer, from Britain's non-membership of the eurozone. If there is any coherent view from the City of the single European currency it is one of hostility rather than advocacy. At a popular level, millions of British tourists and businesspeople travel to the eurozone every year. Some of them certainly conclude that Britain can learn lessons in economic management from its neighbours. But working and taking holidays in the eurozone have not led many Britons to conclude that there is any pressing need for their country to join the euro. Circumstances can certainly be envisaged in which this attitude might change, if the economic performance of the eurozone countries for a substantial period of time outstripped Great Britain's, or perhaps if every other member state of the EU apart from Britain had joined the single currency. But these are in no sense imminent possibilities. While a majority of British electors would still fear the economic consequences of leaving the European Union altogether, no such fear currently attaches in the British electorate to Britain's indefinite absence from the euro.

In the same way as British governmental and public opinion has now concluded that no foreseeable penalty attaches to the preservation of sterling, so they have also concluded more recently that the danger of Britain's political isolation within the European Union has been much exaggerated. When the British government sent Peter Hain as its representative to the European Constitutional Convention in 2002, his mission was at least partly to avoid British isolation within the institutional debates of the Convention. In this context, he was willing to make a number of concessions to other points of view, for instance on the use of the term Constitutional Treaty, on the title of the European Foreign Minister, on the role of the European Parliament, and on the binding character of the Charter of Fundamental Rights. The delay in the signing of the final European Constitutional Treaty was not due to British intransigence, but rather to Spanish and Polish reluctance to accept changes to the Nice Treaty which, at least symbolically, were to their national disadvantage.

It is easy to forget that before the French and Dutch referendums serious commentators, in Britain and elsewhere, considered it a real possibility that the United Kingdom alone might prove unwilling to ratify the Constitutional Treaty. It was no secret that the British government hoped to hold its national referendum on the Treaty as late as possible, allowing as many other countries as possible to ratify the Treaty beforehand. It might then be possible for the government to argue that the referendum was essentially one about Britain's continuing membership of a European Union, on the future structure of which all other member states were agreed. The referendum on the Constitutional Treaty might, on this analysis, become a repetition of the referendum in 1975, with its supposedly clear-cut endorsement of Britain's European future. Blair's failure to hold, let alone win, his much-advertised referendum on the euro would probably have undermined his credibility in trying also to win by such tactics a referendum on the European Constitutional Treaty. Few of his colleagues in the British government seem to have shared his conviction that British voters in 2006 could be persuaded to vote "yes" just as successfully as their parents and younger selves had been in 1975.

All such speculations vanished rapidly from the British debate after the French and Dutch referendums. Some commentators in the United

Kingdom claimed optimistically (from their point of view) that this double rejection of the Treaty marked the beginning of the unravelling of the whole European integrative project. A more general view was that the Treaty was now dead beyond resuscitation and that it was difficult to envisage any remotely similar document for many years in the future. At most, the European Union would be able to agree in the coming decades on discrete limited and incremental changes to its existing institutional structure. The United Kingdom would not necessarily be hostile to such innovations, particularly in areas such as foreign policy and defence, where the British government had a strong hand to play in shaping the terms of the debate towards intergovernmental co-operation and away from further integration through the Union's central institutions. Environmental questions such as climate change are rapidly gaining in political salience both at European and national levels. If a case could be made for institutional change to approach these questions more effectively at European level British public opinion might well be increasingly receptive to such arguments over the coming decade.

Something very like a consensus is emerging that Britain has now arrived at a new point of sustainable equilibrium in its relationship with the rest of the European Union. We will not join the euro for many years, if ever, and it is exceedingly unlikely that the British government will be confronted in the next decade with profound European institutional choices put to it either by all its partners in the Union or even a substantial minority willing to form a hard core. Over the past year, opinion polls in the United Kingdom have shown a noticeable increase in the majorities of British electors supporting British membership of the European Union and believing that the Union is doing its job well. For the United Kingdom to feel in the medium term more at ease with itself in the European Union, a period of minimal institutional change would have much to commend it. Nor need such a period necessarily be a time of complete integrative stagnation. The present functioning of the European Union still contains within itself an immense untapped reservoir of integrative potential. The completion of the single market, the development of the single European currency's governance structure and the vast legislative programme on justice and home affairs are already promising areas of further European integration even without further significant Treaty change. We can confidently say that in ten years' time the European Union will be a much more legislatively and institutionally integrated body than it is today.

The great unresolved question of the European Union is whether the British and the minority of member states in the EU who think as they do will be granted the opportunity they crave for a cessation in the battle between their contrasting and warring fears about the European Union. Whether they are vouchsafed this intermission is largely in the hands of others, not in their own. For better or worse, much of the backdrop for British European policy over the next five years will be set in other European capitals rather than in London. How the British political class and British public opinion will react to the initiatives of others will obviously say much about the legacy left to his successor on European questions by Tony Blair.

The global balance sheet of British public opinion after ten years of New Labour government is a distinctly mixed one in the European sphere. It is probably true that Blair and his colleagues have ensured that Britain will never leave the European Union. Despite the occasional successes in European or local elections of the United Kingdom Independence Party, there is little appetite in the United Kingdom for the economic and political upheaval which would engulf the British Isles in the event of a British withdrawal from the Union. But the price of this relative success has been high. New Labour has easily adapted itself to the moderately eurosceptic rhetoric and policies with which, for instance, John Major came to find himself most at ease. Difficult questions about the European single currency and about the broader course of European integration have either been shelved or treated in the superficial and consequently misleading terms which electoral political convenience demanded. Blair is now fond of polemicising against those who want a "federal European superstate" and presenting himself as an ardent defender of British sovereignty. These empty phrases do no justice to the difficult but vital decisions with which Britain may be confronted over the coming years in its European diplomacy. To remain indefinitely outside the single European currency, for instance, will be to take by default a decision having the profoundest consequences for the United Kingdom's role within the European Union. Farfetched speculation about the supposedly imminent demise of the eurozone is no substitute for hard-headed consideration of the real political and economic consequences for this country of increasing marginalisation from the economic integration which is the core task of the European Union.

In truth, over the past ten years New Labour has pursued a risky but electorally successful game with the European issue. It has employed a sufficiently pro-European rhetoric, particularly outside the United

Kingdom, to differentiate itself from its Conservative opponents. However, it has been acutely aware that Conservative euroscepticism reflects one part of the schizophrenic views of the European Union which are so prevalent in the British electorate. There have always been definite limits to the willingness of the present Labour government to present itself, or be seen, as a pro-European administration. Gordon Brown in particular has never been shy of improving his personal standing with the British eurosceptic press by repeated criticisms of the allegedly encrusted and inflexible European social model. The outcome of the past decade has been paradoxical. Britain is today as firmly anchored in the European Union as it has ever been, but is probably less inclined than it has ever been to participate in any further substantial integrative progress of the Union. Nothing remotely resembling the moribund European Constitutional Treaty could now stand any chance of endorsement in a British referendum. Whether initiatives from others will force Britain again over the short term to confront difficult European questions can only be a matter of speculation. The proposals of Sarkozy for a much reduced version of the Constitutional Treaty might appear to some British commentators an encouraging initial sign, even if his proposed reduced treaty would still be unacceptable to current British public opinion. If Britain is able over the next two or three years to persuade its European partners that the whole concept of a European Constitutional Treaty should be abandoned (and Britain will not be the only member state making this argument), then it may well be that the British government and electorate will be content to acquiesce in marginal changes to the existing European treaties which can be represented as the tidying-up exercise which Peter Hain claimed to discern in the Constitutional Treaty. From the British perspective, such favoured areas of change would no doubt include the non-rotating Presidency of the European Council, reweighting of votes in the Council, some small increase in qualified majority voting and tighter institutional arrangements for the Common Foreign and Security Policy.

If any substantial body of EU member states show themselves, however, set upon any more substantial integrative initiatives over the coming years, Britain emphatically will not be one of them. Britain's contradictory fears about European integration are at the moment largely dormant. If aroused by ambitious new integrative initiatives from others, these conflicting fears will probably not be resolved in the short term in the way they traditionally have been in the past. Forced to choose, the British electorate and political class of today are more fearful of national submersion in the European Union than of isolation from the Union. This is a novelty which perhaps as yet is insufficiently understood in the rest of the European Union. Britain's remaining without obvious financial penalty for so long outside the euro and the double failure of the Constitutional Treaty in France and the Netherlands have greatly altered the British perception of risk and reward associated with their participation in the European Union. Much will need to change in the rest of the European Union and in Britain for the terms of the British equation to be reconstructed. There are many in Britain who believe that such changes, notably along the lines of a successful core Europe, are unachievable. Others recall that most British observers thought exactly the same at the time of the Messina Conference. Since then, it has always been tempting for British elite opinion to believe that the integrative urge of their European neighbours has reached its zenith. John Major and his Foreign Secretary Douglas Hurd zealously if bizarrely promoted this interpretation of the Maastricht Treaty, thereby storing up for themselves an enormous reservoir of disappointed expectations. In recent months, New Labour has shown signs of wanting to go down the same primrose path, smugly believing that Europe's integrative momentum is ebbing if not disappearing. If, like their predecessors, Tony Blair and Gordon Brown are wrong in this analysis, then the consequences for Britain and for its partners in the European Union will be as profound as they are, in the long term, unpredictable.

Part Three

Britain, Security and a Federal Europe

There has been a tendency for much of the debate about Europe to focus on what Britain is giving, or rather giving up, through membership of the Union. Alongside the myth that the Community was conceived as, or claimed to be, or should be, no more than an economic organisation for freeing trade, this has resulted in a national failure to envisage the gains – actual and potential – from membership of what is now the Union. Can we begin after more than 30 years' membership of the Community and the Union to envisage ourselves as a part of a European polity and assess that polity in terms of offering solutions to our own problems and concerns?

Amongst current British preoccupations are the health of our own democratic political institutions and a cluster of external international issues confronting every European state. Europe-wide political parties contesting elections and seeking to influence policy choices throughout the Union would be a vital concomitant, and would give added value to British constitutional and political life. In the wider international sphere, and whatever the future may hold, the current pre-eminence of the US is an unsatisfactory basis for a safer and more secure world. For Britain Europe offers an essential route for achieving our own major international goals including the resolution of key climate issues. Externally, and given the necessary mechanisms and instrumentalities, Europe can underpin the security we all crave through making a major contribution towards resolving global problems.

Chapter 7

Might EU-wide Parties Help Revive Britain's Ailing Democracy?

John Palmer

IN A LITTLE-NOTICED DEVELOPMENT EARLIER THIS YEAR the European Parliament passed, by massive majorities and with the backing of all the major political groups, resolutions designed to give legal, political and financial expression to the creation of fully-fledged transnational European political parties.

The proposals passed by the EP could open the way for voters in all EU countries to choose from the same lists of candidates put forward by European political parties. Individuals would be able to join the European parties - which would have a central role in European referendums and in the election of the Commission President. The Parliament also called for EU legislation and endorsed financial reforms to assist the parties in developing beyond umbrella organisations for national parties. MEPs suggested an increase in the funding shared between European parties last year, to take account of EU enlargement and increased operational costs. Other measures approved by the European Parliament include the development of European political foundations and support for European parties' youth organisations.

The intention is to help bridge the gulf which has developed between the electorates in member states and the European Union institutions. But could the promised emergence of European-wide parties also help to restore life to ailing national democracies in EU member states? To pose the question is to invite the ridicule of sections of the British intellectual and political elite. Politics at the European level – the "realist" argument goes – is destined to handle only marginal, largely technocratic, issues mainly to do with running the single market. Better, it is said, to bury the goal of a serious transnational European democracy along with that of closer European integration and focus instead on the real politics in the member states. The only serious democratic debate, we are assured, takes place at the level of the nations, within their parliaments and through their political parties.

Leaving aside some possible misunderstandings about nation-state and member state in modern Europe, this ignores what is happening both within the EU and to national politics throughout Europe. Despite the disarray over the constitutional treaty and the future of EU governance, member state governments continue to thrust greater responsibilities on the Union. There is, of course, a worrying contradiction here: governments impose ever more ambitious policy objectives for the EU but they are reluctant to give it the means to achieve them.

Secondly the realists seem strangely unaware of the direct link between the growth of public cynicism about national politics and the relentless draining from national political discourse of any real sense of choice about issues of major political importance. The national political debate in most western democracies is now primarily focused around secondary issues – essentially disagreements over the micromanagement of policy strategies. There is a broad – even asphyxiating – consensus between the parties about the strategies themselves.

The gradual disappearance of strategic differences between the mainstream political parties – not only in Britain, but throughout much of the democratic world – is in turn eroding the links between parties and their supporters. The main beneficiaries of the resulting mood of cynicism in many countries are likely to be populist and racist parties on the far right. The threatened breakthrough by the neo-fascist British National Party in local elections may be a case in point. The loans-for-peerages scandal in Britain only really makes sense when it is placed into the context of this wider crisis of the party system. The resort to secretive - and potentially corrupt - forms of funding is a direct consequence of a dramatic collapse in membership of political parties and a virtual implosion of core activist membership.

Party members have been particularly alienated by the steady erosion of internal democracy and the replacement of traditions of local activist campaigning by focus groups, spin doctoring and hugely expensive media campaigns run by remote party bureaucracies. The migration from the party of much its activist core has reached the point where many local Labour Parties are now unable or ineligible even to send delegates to advisory policy conferences.

There are those who believe we are headed to some kind of post-political society. But might a new kind of democracy emerge where substitutes for parties and the role they have played will be found in new institutions of consultation and decision-making? Alternatively, might the emergence of democratic politics at the supranational level – first in the European Union and eventually globally – breathe new life into the parties by creating space for them to offer voters substantially different choices about the future kind of economic and social system in which we wish to live?

The answer may be a mixture of the two. If they are to remain relevant in the face not only of globalisation, but also given the profound changes in traditional patterns of class society, the acceleration of the information revolution and the emergence of new social forces, parties will have to undergo radical reconstruction. The days when tightly knit groups of professional, bureaucratic and political elites run major parties, effectively dispensing with active members and relying primarily on media promotion, are surely drawing to a close.

The elites now increasingly preside over shell-like parties devoid of anything resembling mass membership. If they are to survive, parties are going to have to explore new links with broader civil society forces, discover new ways of empowering their members, and learn to pursue political goals which will have to be enacted as much at the supranational level as at the national or regional levels. The generally declining trend in voter participation in elections (national as well as European) is alarming. The recent Italian election was a striking exception to this general rule. But voter turnout in Italy may well be reduced in future if the resulting deadlock between the two major centre-right and centre-left coalitions – whose concrete policy disagreements are very limited - produces disillusion with the hope for radical reform.

Opinion polls across Europe reveal a startling erosion of public confidence in national democratic systems, irrespective of the political orientation of specific governments. Why should voters feel so disenchanted with their national parties and political institutions? An important part of the answer is that governments are increasingly perceived by the public as impotent in the face of globalisation. Governments - and hence parties vying for national office - are seen as marginal actors in the dramas played out when global economic pressures impact on national economies, patterns of employment and traditional social and welfare policies.

Restricted in the range of strategies they might wish to follow in pursuing economic, social and environmental objectives by the fear of loss of global competitiveness, parties feel obliged to fight elections in an ever diminishing political space in the electoral middle ground. Mainstream political parties everywhere are being pushed into more or less the same ideological telephone box. The fragmentation of traditional political loyalties has made the outcome of elections even more unpredictable as voters lose the habits and loyalties of a lifetime. Meanwhile the national political debate increasingly focuses on relatively marginal points of difference between the parties - MPs report that on the ground only micro-local issues are seen as politically relevant by voters. This often leaves them as little more than surrogate local councillors. Voters are increasingly alienated by the exaggerated rhetoric and hype that surrounds the few residual differences between the national parties. The alienation towards the mainstream parties felt by the young in particular may explain why so many, who in the past would have wanted to pursue their ideals through party political involvement, have deserted them for single-issue campaigns and NGOs. However throughout Europe radical rightist, protectionist and racist populist parties on the fringes of the political system seem likely to be the main beneficiaries of this continuing alienation of the electorates.

Ironically the emergence of transnational European Union political parties may offer a means of revitalising democratic choice. The global market will always impose some restrictions on policy choices while also offering important new economic opportunities. But the sheer size and relative economic self-sufficiency of a European Union of 27 states willing to pool sovereignty and act together means that through action at EU level parties could offer voters a much wider range of policy alternatives. At present there is a big difference between the responses to globalisation of mainstream politicians in Britain, in France and in the Nordic countries for example. But if the Nordic approach rather than post-Thatcherite neo-liberalism is to triumph in the longer run it cannot remain restricted to a small number of countries and must become the basis for EU strategy. Throughout Europe political leaders remain trapped within the shrinking horizons of their purely national debates. They have not given voters any reasons for thinking that - by acting together at the European level - it may be possible to achieve objectives that otherwise remain illusory at the national level. They had better learn to do so and soon.

There is, of course, a widespread assumption in Britain that the underlying process of European integration has come to a halt and may even have begun to go into reverse. Even a normally well-informed observer such as the editor of Prospect magazine, David Goodhart, draws the conclusion that, at best, politics at the European Union level will always be left with relatively minor, largely technocratic, responsibilities for running a single European market. Writing for The Guardian blog site *Commentisfree* he complains of:

"A problem here that few pro-Europeans seem to grasp: Europe is a second-order institution. The main political reality now and for the foreseeable future remains national. It cannot be repeated often enough how, come election time, almost all the things that British citizens really care about – tax and spend, the NHS, education, pensions, crime and anti-social behaviour, immigration and foreign policy – are still overwhelmingly determined at national level."

The European Union certainly faces serious governance problems which risk being exacerbated as the EU continues to enlarge. The Union's capacity to manage its existing responsibilities is matched by the weak democratic accountability of the EU institutions to the voting public. In particular the Council of Ministers – representing member state governments – is subject to scant democratic control. Those problems can only get worse the longer the kind of institutional reforms outlined in the constitutional treaty are delayed. But member state governments are determined to impose ever greater responsibilities on the Union. In economic reform, justice and internal security, foreign policy and external security, in defence procurement and – most recently – in energy policy, governments want the Union to do more – not less. While it is true that health, education and pensions remain matters of overwhelmingly national responsibility (although in many cases devolved from the national to regional government) most of the other policies mentioned by Goodhart are – to a greater or lesser extent – already a matter of "shared competence" between the member states and the Union. Too often, however, they escape proper scrutiny by either national parliaments or the European Parliament.

Most of the new areas of EU responsibility involve decision-making based on intergovernmental co-operation rather than through supranational EU law. But governments have already agreed that some important aspects of justice and internal security policy should become subject to supranational decision-making because intergovernmental co-operation has failed to deliver hoped-for results. Given the painfully slow pace of progress in economic reform and social cohesion and the disparity between the ambitious objectives of a common energy policy and the modesty of the means chosen to deliver it, similar conclusions may eventually also be drawn in these areas.

There is no real "Chinese Wall" separating European Union decisions taken through intergovernmental co-operation and those decisions taken through Community law. One has only to look at the handling of foreign policy challenges, which involve both "hard" and "soft" security, to understand why the EU institutions have had to be brought into the decision-making process by national governments. Member states can deliver troops on the ground to deal with crisis situations. But to deliver supportive "soft" security policies on aid, economic development and trade policies, they need decisions by the supranational EU institutions. The suggestion, therefore, that European democratic politics must remain a chimera because the EU does not take important-enough decisions is distinctly odd.

Until recently the political groups in the European Parliament, which described themselves as parties, were little more than loose confederations of national parties with (greater or lesser) ambitions to become fully-fledged transnational parties. But they now seem serious about achieving full transnational party status.

It remains to be seen whether EU governments will agree to the reforms proposed by the European Parliament. The basis for individual membership of European-wide parties must be settled. However parties have already had to confront a similar problem with regional devolution. Specifically regional parties – many linked to their political family at the level of the state - have emerged and established a considerable degree of autonomy. There appears to be no valid reason why this should not be the case with the European parties. However they have yet to establish their autonomy and their own identity – vis-à-vis their constituent national parties - in those policy areas that are properly the business of the European Union.

At this point the "realists" retort that the European Union itself is suffering from a profound democratic malaise – as instanced by poor voter turnout in European Parliament elections. The realists are right. There is a widespread feeling that EU decision-makers – most especially member state governments - are not being properly held to democratic account. But voters are understandably confused about the division of responsibilities between regional, national and European levels of governance. They have no clear understanding about who is responsible for what – and who is accountable to whom – within the EU decision-making architecture.

The real question about low voting levels in European elections is why so many go to the polls at all when the consequences of voting in the EP elections appear so marginal. European Parliament elections are invariably fought almost exclusively on second-hand, purely domestic, issues. Voters are asked to pass judgement about their national administrations, although European elections have no impact on who governs in any member state. European elections are simply not about enough at present to capture the imagination and enthusiasm of the electorate. A vote in the European Parliament election has no executive outcome. National and regional assembly voters can elect or dismiss governments. A vote in the EP election elects neither the President of the Commission (one key part of the European executive) nor the President of the Council of Ministers (the other part of the EU executive). The wonder is that voting in European elections has remained so high.

The Constitutional Treaty would have strengthened the democratic accountability of the Council of Ministers – not least by requiring it to pass all laws in public instead of behind closed doors. But further reforms are urgently needed. In modern European democracies the public also expects not only to be consulted but also directly to elect the decision-making executives. If there is to be a reworking of the Constitutional Treaty, it should strengthen the provision for the election of future Commission Presidents through the European Parliament. The emerging European Union political parties could then nominate their preferred candidate for the post of Commission President as part of their European Parliament election campaigns in 2009.

All of this will involve an unambiguous politicisation of the Commission. It is true that in the past the Commission has been most influential when it has acted consensually and above party politics. But the European Union has now evolved to the extent that citizens must be able to make their strategic political choices knowing how this will affect the kind of leadership of the EU institutions. This should involve elections not just for the Commission President but also the proposed EU President of the European Council – who presumably would play a head of state role for the Union.

This politicisation is already starting to make itself felt within the European Commission. It is being reinforced by the more overtly political character of the present Commission led by Jose-Manuel Barroso. The electoral shift to the right and centre right in elections across the EU in recent years and the disappearance of the second Commissioner from the larger member states, usually drawn from the opposition, has produced an overwhelmingly right-wing Commission. In the longer run, however, this *de facto* politicisation will be healthy. The role of the Parliament as co-legislator with the Council of Ministers has grown with successive EU Treaties. Since the last European election research shows that in their voting behaviour MEPs are motivated less by national loyalties and more by transnational party political and ideological differences.

In a study of changes in European Parliament voting patterns, Simon Hix, Professor of European and Comparative Politics at the London School of Economics, states:

"... on the positive side, and potentially far more profound, is the emergence of a genuine 'democratic party system' in the European Parliament. First, voting in the Parliament is more along transnational and ideological party lines than along national lines, and increasingly so. The main European parties in the Parliament – such as the European People's Party (EPP), the Party of European Socialists (PES), and the Alliance of Liberals and Democrats for Europe (ALDE) – are now more 'cohesive' in their voting behaviour than the Democrats and Republicans in the US Congress. Second, competition and coalition-formation between the parties in the Parliament is increasingly along left-right lines, with the 'grand coalition' between the PES and EPP gradually giving way to shifting centre-left or centre-right majority legislative coalitions.

These developments are quite remarkable when one considers that voting in the other main EU legislative institution (the Council) is primarily along national lines, and that the parties in the European Parliament are not forced by a 'government' to 'back them or sack them', which is why parties in national parliaments are generally highly cohesive."

It is too soon to be sure whether the emerging European political parties will be able to establish their competitive ideological territories with sufficient clarity to give voters a real sense of choice in the 2009 European Parliament election. Important divisions are beginning to emerge between the major EP parties on issues such as the future of the European economic and social model, the services directive and the weight to be given to environmental sustainability in EU economic strategy.

Foreign and security policy is still clearly a matter for intergovernmental co-operation between member states and does not fall within the classical legal scope of EU Community law (although other important elements of external policy do). But with EU governments increasingly acting together in the field of foreign and security policy neither national parliaments nor the European Parliament are able to hold governments properly to account. One possibility, in these areas of hybrid responsibility shared by national and EU governance, might be to give representatives of both national parliaments and the European Parliament joint powers of invigilation and policy approval.

If democratic politics at the European level is to become a reality, the elected European Parliament must be given eventual equality in terms of colegislative powers with the Council of Ministers. It is also unhealthy that the European Parliament has an important voice in determining how EU revenue is spent, but no powers to raise revenue. However the planned mid-term review of the 2007-13 financial perspectives due to be held in 2008-9 will provide the European political parties with an important opportunity to open a long-overdue debate about European taxation and expenditure. It will take years – maybe decades – before a European demos comes to full fruition. But a start to the creation of a European Union transnational democracy should not be delayed. The creation of a European demos will not threaten democracy at the national, regional or local level. Rather it will reinforce the accountability of all levels of governance.

Chapter 8

Britain, Security and a Federal Europe

John Pinder

THE EUROPEAN COMMUNITY WAS FOUNDED to meet what world war two had shown to be Europeans' existential need for security and peace among the member states; and it was developed, largely to this end, through federal steps towards economic integration. Both purposes required elements of common government because both are subject to cross-frontier forces, beyond the scope of traditional intergovernmental relationships to manage. Yet contemporary European states were not ready to create a federal constitution as the Americans did in 1789. So elements of federal institutions and powers have been established during the past half century through a step-by-step process, to deal with specific requirements, while at the same time transforming relations between the member states so that war between them has become unthinkable.

This process has not been ineluctable. Each main step has required political will. This was forthcoming, not just for economic advantage but also because leaders of the founding states, together with substantial sections of the people, remained conscious of the appalling damage that could be done if cross-frontier forces were not subject to adequate governance. The Community's founders took the initiative in this direction, unprecedented among modern nation-states, because they were acutely conscious of this need and aware of the capacity of federal principles to deal with it in an effective and democratic way. Their lead has drawn others in this direction, to the point where a large proportion of European states now participate in what has been developed into the European Union.

This example of the application of federal principles to relations among states has already been influential in some other parts of the world and there can be little doubt that its influence will continue to grow. But, even after half a century of stepwise development, the Union remains quite far short of being fully effective and democratic. Sadly, it must be recognised that Britain has played a largely negative part, serving to delay, weaken or prevent the steps in a federal direction, save for the very important project of establishing the single market and for respecting the rule of Community law.

The argument in this paper is that the root cause of Britain's negative role has been a failure to appreciate the fundamental significance of the contribution to security of the development of federal institutions, which remains important in the still-enlarging Union following German unification and is increasingly essential for Europe's role in a very dangerous world. This hostility to federal developments reflects a failure to take the measure of the great forces, powers and problems that predominate in the world and hence to help shape the destiny of Europe, including of course Britain, and the world around it. The hostility to federalism and the accompanying failure to recognise the weakness of intergovernmental co-operation also reflect a lack of respect for, and even of interest in, essential elements of British political culture, which in fact played a leading part in the evolution of federal thinking.

Britain's role in developing the federal idea

A federal European Union is often presented as the product of foreign political theory imposed on the practical British by continental Europeans. In the federal development of the European Union the idea has, to the contrary, been a product of largely British political ideas and practice. The genius of the American Founding Fathers - British people displaced across the Atlantic - was based on British liberal political philosophy and pragmatic ability to solve political problems in ways acceptable to the main interests involved. This enabled them to discover how to combine the self-government of states with shared government to meet common cross-frontier needs beyond the capacity of intergovernmental co-operation to handle, which could be done only by applying principles of liberal democracy, with representative government together with rule of law based on citizens' rights, at the levels of both states and federation.[1]

It was the Westminster Parliament that later enacted the Canadian and Australian federal constitutions. Following Tocqueville's outstanding *Democracy in America*, moreover, eminent British scholars played a leading part in developing the federal idea in the second half of the nineteenth century.[2] *Bryce's American Constitution* was for half a century seen on both sides of the Atlantic as the classic work on the subject.[3] The application of the federal idea to the internal reform of centralised states, developed by Acton, influenced Gladstone's policy of home rule for Ireland and was taken up by Winston Churchill in 1912 in a more general proposal for reform of the United Kingdom.[4]

Seeley's proposal for imperial federation has been largely forgotten, perhaps partly because the British no longer wish to be reminded of their imperial past. It has been brought back into focus largely through the work of Professor Michael Burgess.[5] However, Seeley's idea is strikingly relevant to the problem of world governance in an age dominated by superpowers. For his aim was not a crude enhancement of British power for its own sake, but rather a federation of Britain with the self-governing Dominions in order to forestall domination of the world by the two emerging superpowers, the United States and Russia. Although domination by the United States and the Soviet Union has been superseded by the US as the sole superpower, China is now emerging to take the Soviet Union's place; and, even if India may be not more than a decade or two behind, a European federation could perform the role envisaged by Seeley for the imperial federation. Seeley did in fact consider whether Europe could play that part. Reasonably enough in 1871 in the wake of the Franco-Prussian war, he thought it was not feasible. He had, however, demonstrated in a little-known article that a European federation would be the way to ensuring that such wars would never recur.[6] Leading British academics seem to have been more apt then to think such bold thoughts than most are today.

It was in the late 1930s that British federalists attained outstanding significance in the development of the federal idea in Europe.[7] Federal Union, founded in reaction against the Munich agreement, received editorial support in *The Times, The Guardian* and *The New Statesman*, and membership reached 10,000, with over 200 branches throughout the country. In June 1940 when the War Cabinet approved the idea of a union with France it contained three members, Clement Attlee, Ernest Bevin and Sir Archibald Sinclair, who had declared their support for the federal idea.[8] Churchill was to write of his surprise to see "the staid, solid, experienced politicians engage themselves so passionately in an immense design";[9] and John Colville, his Assistant Private Secretary, wrote the next day in his diary that "we had before us the bridge to a new world, the first elements of European and even World Federation."[10]

There were books and pamphlets by such luminaries as William Beveridge, Ivor Jennings, Lord Lothian, Lionel Bobbins and Barbara Wootton. The prevention of war was their predominant motive, as it was that of the authors who had the most influence in securing popular support. Penguin sold over 100,000 copies of William Curry's *The Case for Federal Union* within six months of publication.[11] He had been much influenced by the American

Clarence Streit's *Union Now*, in which he made a powerful case for a federation of the democracies on both sides of the Atlantic.[12] This was undermined by American isolationism. Curry concluded with a call for European federation. Lothian's *Pacifism is not Enough, nor Patriotism Either* was perhaps more permanently influential. He made a brilliant general case for federation as the way to prevent war.[13] Indeed it was with the approach and outbreak of war that the idea of a European federation, starting with Britain, France and other European democracies, became more prominent.[14]

Lionel Robbins, a distinguished liberal economist, exemplified this trend, demonstrating at the same time the relationship between the economic and the security motives for federation. He was deeply critical of the protectionism that blighted the capitalist economies in the 1930s and regarded an international market as essential for a developed economy. But he affirmed in his *National Planning and International Order* that it must be subject to the international rule of law and hence to an international court. Since the laws would have to develop in order to meet evolving economic needs, an international legislature would also be required: hence the need for an international federal system.[15] In his *Economic Causes of War*, completed just after the outbreak of war in September 1939, he demonstrated the relationship between the economic and security purposes of federal government. He concluded with a passionate appeal for the war to be followed by a peace in which the great German people, purged of Nazism, would become free and equal citizens of the United States of Europe.[16]

Economic and security motives in Europe's federal development

Security and the power relationships closely related to it have been the basic motive for substantial shifts towards combining separate self-government with shared government, as Daniel Elazar described the design of federation.[17] With the shift in the 1950s from security to economics as the explicit motive for federal steps, the British, when they finally did accede, were able to ignore the motive of security and hence also the need for any shift towards shared government that would touch on what they saw as desirable elements of sovereignty, widely interpreted. So they resisted reforms designed to make the institutions more democratic and effective, such as more majority voting in the Council of Ministers, codecision for the European Parliament or strengthening the Commission.

Ironically enough, it was Robbins's books, mainly on the economic grounds for federation, that appear to have influenced Altiero Spinelli the most when British federalist literature inspired him to devote the rest of his life to the cause of a federal Europe. Recalling, many years later, the impact on him of the British federalists' literature, he was to write that their "analysis of the political and economic perversion that nationalism leads to, and their reasoned presentation of the federalist alternative, have remained to this day impressed on my memory like a revelation."[18] Robbins's two books were cited the most frequently by Spinelli in his writings whilst in confinement in Ventotene;[19] and it was surely the final chapter of *The Economic Causes of War*, explicitly connecting the security with the economic motives in its political advocacy of a European federation, which influenced him the most. Nonetheless, it was Jean Monnet who launched the first major step towards a federal Europe, also combining the fundamental motive of security, in the form of permanent peace among France, Germany and neighbouring countries, with that of economic efficiency. Already in 1943, soon after he had arrived in Algiers to join the Comité de Libération Nationale, Etienne Hirsch asked him why he was poring over a map. Monnet pointed to the area between France and Germany which contained their principal production of coal and steel, and said that so long as this remained under the control of the French and German governments there would always be wars between them. So it would have to be removed from their control.[20]

Whilst this seemed to Hirsch to be utopian at the time, Monnet saw his opportunity early in 1950. As head of the Commissariat du Plan, he had responsibilities for both the coal and steel industries. The Americans and British, whose occupation zones included the Ruhr, decided to lift the limit on steel production so as to enable the Germans to start their economy working normally again. This touched an extremely raw French nerve, given the potential of steel as the industrial basis for military power. Monnet was convinced that the French must not try to place the Germans in an inferior position, as they had done after 1918 with disastrous consequences. So he proposed the establishment of a High Authority to be responsible for governance of the two countries' coal and steel industries, with French and Germans equally represented on it. This was the basis for French Foreign Minister Robert Schuman's Declaration on 7 May 1950, backed by the French and German governments, whose central element was the High Authority, independent of the governments, to take over from them control of the two sectors. The Declaration stated explicitly that it was intended to "lay the first concrete foundation for a European federation."[21]

While the merger of markets made economic sense, to the French and Germans its profound significance was to entrench an altogether new relationship as the basis for permanent peace, by transferring responsibility for the industrial sinews of war from their separate rule to genuinely shared rule. The British government on the other hand, having regained confidence in national sovereignty following success in the war, was not willing to take such a radical step towards shared rule in order to build a new relationship among European states. The Home Secretary, Herbert Morrison, reacted succinctly: "It's no good. The Durham miners wouldn't wear it."²²

Monnet chaired the conference of representatives of the six founder states - France, Germany, Italy, Belgium, the Netherlands and Luxembourg - charged with drafting the treaty establishing the European Coal and Steel Community. Being familiar with the weaknesses of intergovernmental co-operation, as Deputy Secretary General of the League of Nations and head of the Anglo-French procurement boards in both world wars, his central objective was to make the High Authority an effective European executive, responsible to Community institutions, not to the several member state governments.

Monnet was favourably disposed to the idea of federal government, strongly recommending *The Federalist* of Hamilton, Jay and Madison to the Secretary of the Comité de Libération Nationale in 1943 and subsequently keeping it constantly on his desk as President of the High Authority.²³ He was not familiar with the constitutional detail, so it was appropriate that Adenauer appointed Walter Hallstein, who was a distinguished academic jurist versed in federal constitutions, to lead the German negotiators. Whilst others certainly contributed to the design of the Community institutions, Hallstein's participation guaranteed that the foundations would be laid for the development of a complete system of federal government. As he put it in addresses in Frankfurt and Washington after the conclusion of the negotiations, the High Authority was a federal executive with governmental powers over the coal and steel sectors, the Council corresponded to a federal House of the States, the Common Assembly was the forerunner of a European Parliament and the Court of Justice had the functions of a constitutional court, an administrative court and a court of appeal in disputes between the High Authority and the member states.²⁴ That was indeed the direction in which the European Community, later the European Union, was to develop by steps and stages, with periodical breakthroughs and setbacks, during the subsequent 55 years.

Britain's initial refusal

British reluctance to participate in the foundation of the Community was not surprising, given the effect of the war on relations with the Americans and with continental Europeans. However, hostility to the federal idea as such does not seem to have been inevitable. With Churchill's immense prestige after his wartime performance, his speech in September 1946 in Zurich, advocating "a kind of United States of Europe," had an electrifying effect on the Continent. Only just over a year after the end of the war he said that the "first step in the re-creation of the European family must be a partnership between France and Germany .... There can be no revival of Europe without a spiritually great France and a spiritually great Germany. The structure of the United States of Europe, if well and truly built, will be such as to make the material strength of a single state less important."[25]

If this initiated the process that led continental states towards the foundation of the ECSC it might surely have been expected to have some lasting resonance at home. But two-party politics intervened: the Labour government instructed Labour MPs to boycott the Congress of Europe at The Hague, over which Churchill presided in May 1948 and which representatives of other democratic left-wing parties attended in force. It set a precedent for the tradition of adversarial politics to impede attempts to pursue pro-European policies.

Just before the Hague Congress, however, R. W. G. Mackay, a former chairman of Federal Union who was by then a Labour MP, secured 100 Labour signatures to a motion calling for a constituent assembly to "draw up a constitution for a European Federation"; Robert Boothby persuaded a similar number of Conservative MPs to sign. Prime Minister Attlee, in responding to the motion, expressed his belief that "federation must eventually come" - but evidently not yet.[26] People in key positions in the Labour Party as well as Foreign Office officials were against the idea of a federal Europe. Anthony Eden, who was to be Foreign Secretary in Churchill's government after the Conservatives won the 1951 elections, was implacably opposed. Underlying the aversion of many such people to the federal idea were adherence to a classical view of international relations and, following the Suez episode in 1956, almost unqualified dependence on the bilateral relationship with the United States, at the expense of any idea of building the effective European partner that Monnet envisaged for the Atlantic relationship.

Leading academics specialising in the subject lent support to the British focus on economic rather than the security motives that were fundamental for the development of the Community's institutions. The neo-functionalist theory which, together with various successors such as liberal inter-governmentalism, has remained very influential, omitted to explain why the ECSC with its supranational institutions was established in the first place and hence neglected the considerations relating to security which were to retain their motive power.[27] In 1984 Alan Milward sought, on the basis of a massive economic analysis, to belittle Monnet's achievement, claiming that he was "an assiduous self-publicist and a remarkable collector of disciples" who had merely sought advantage for the French steel industry through a plan that was "the crudest possible expression of mercantilist principles."[28] His book contained a vast quantity of economic material and analysis, which served to reinforce the British illusion that the Community was merely an economic device, neglecting the evidence that the primary purpose had been to remove the possibility of war among the states; and it is consequently not surprising that, by ignoring the strength of the security motive which was fundamental to the French and German commitment to the single currency project, he predicted in his second big book on the Community, written shortly before the Maastricht Treaty was signed, that the monetary union would not be established.[29]

Given this ingrained resistance, in official doctrine and much mainstream academic work, to viewing the EC/EU as more than an economic device without fundamental implications for sovereignty, it is not surprising that the British have been systematically obstructive in the development of the institutions beyond the intergovernmental and that the single market is the only major project to which they have given their wholehearted commitment.

From Defence Community to Economic Community

In June 1950, just as the negotiations on the ECSC Treaty began, North Korea invaded South Korea. The United States transferred troops from Germany to Korea, demanding that their replacement be by Germans in order to maintain the defensive capacity against the Soviet threat, recently manifested by the Berlin blockade. This touched an even more sensitive nerve for the French than had the revival of the German steel industry and Monnet feared that it would derail the ECSC negotiations. Consequently he proposed to the Prime Minister, René Pleven, to initiate the project of a European army, with a European Defence Community along the lines proposed for coal and steel. This was, he felt, equivalent to a premature move to a European federation, but better than abandoning the process of constructing a federation when it had only just begun.[30] When agreement on the Treaty establishing the ECSC was secured, he wrote a note to clarify his own thinking which specified the future steps as "single market, single currency, Federation."[31]

Meanwhile Spinelli had built a strong federalist movement in Italy and formed a close relationship with Ivan Matteo Lombardo, Minister for Europe in Alcide De Gasperi's government. Drawing on his intensive study of "Hamiltonian" federalism, Spinelli wrote a paper explaining that a European army would have to be responsible to a democratic European government. This made a deep impression on De Gasperi, who persuaded the governments of the other five states which were by then about to establish the ECSC that a European Political Community would be required as the political counterpart of the EDC.[32] Monnet, likewise impressed by Spinelli's argument, suggested that its constitution be drafted by the Common Assembly, as the parliamentary institution of the ECSC was called.[33] They persuaded Paul-Henri Spaak, the Belgian Foreign Minister, to commit himself to the project and he became the President of both the newly established Assembly and the closely related drafting body.[34] Spinelli judged that, while the resulting draft EPC Treaty was not fully federal, it would be a good basis for further efforts to complete the federal process.[35] Whilst the EDC Treaty had been signed by all six Community states and ratified by Germany and the Benelux countries, the political strength of the opposition to it in France had increased, with the election of more Gaullist deputies in the Assemblée Nationale alongside the numerous Communists. So French ratification depended on the socialists, of whom about half would not vote in favour of the EDC without British support to counterbalance the German membership. They may well have felt entitled to expect such support from Churchill's government, since one of the starting points for the EDC project had been the resolution initiated by Churchill in the Assembly of the Council of Europe in which he called for "the immediate establishment of a united European armed force" in which "we would all play an honourable and active part." Nor did he demur when others added to the resolution that the force would be under the authority of a European Minister of Defence and subject to European democratic control.[36] But Churchill was now old and sick and preferred to leave the issue to Eden. The latter was not only hostile to British participation but also to any support for the project in the form of a commitment to keep British troops on the Continent, which might well have been enough to secure the necessary socialist votes. So in August 1954 the Assemblée Nationale refused to ratify the EDC Treaty; and Eden inspired the setting up of the toothless Western European Union, bolstered by the commitment to keep a substantial British force on the Continent. This was widely seen in Britain as a triumph for British diplomacy; and it certainly put an end to the direct approach to European federation through integration of defence and encouraged British hopes that federal development of the Community had come to a stop.

Here again, however, the British failed to appreciate the strength of support among the founding states for continued development of the Community as the framework to ensure peaceful relations among them, even though the direct assault on the military citadel of national sovereignty had been frustrated. The process of federal development through Community institutions resumed with the establishment in 1958 of the European Economic Community, extending this form of governance to a general common market, and Euratom designed to do the same for the peaceful uses of atomic energy. Even though the Commission was a somewhat less independent executive than the ECSC's High Authority, the EEC greatly enhanced the power of Community institutions through the much wider scope of their responsibilities. At the same time it reinforced the British view that the Community was an economic organisation lacking the strategic significance which could motivate a more radical approach to national sovereignty.

In turn, however, this confronted the British for the first time with the fear of economic disadvantage and loss of political influence through exclusion from the developing Common Market. The election of General de Gaulle as French President shortly after the Rome Treaties entered into force reassured them on the grounds that he would have no truck with federalism. Their confidence was misguided on two counts: first, in 1961 de Gaulle vetoed Britain's first attempt to accede; second, although he remained President until 1969 and Britain did not accede until 1973, the desire to continue federal developments remained strong thereafter. De Gaulle regarded the Common Market itself with some favour, as good medicine for the French economy and, with the common agricultural policy, useful for the French national interest. But he was fundamentally opposed to federal elements in the institutions and even threatened the Community's existence in 1965 when he instructed his ministers to boycott the Council while he sought to block the introduction of qualified majority voting that the Treaty stipulated. De Gaulle also wanted to prevent the European Parliament, as the Community's Assembly was to be called, from being granted any power over the agricultural budget and to reduce the Commission's role to that of a secretariat. In short he wanted to strip the Community of its federal elements and turn it into a routine intergovernmental organisation. The other five member states resisted his demands but had to accept that powers for the Parliament would have to await his departure, whilst the unanimity rule would remain the practice in the Council until the 1980s.

After de Gaulle: half a century of federal developments

Following de Gaulle's resignation in 1969, his successor Georges Pompidou retained many of his policies but was more willing to negotiate. In December 1969 he agreed that negotiations on British entry could begin, provided that the agricultural price was paid and the principle of monetary union was accepted. Edward Heath, who became Prime Minister in 1971 when negotiations for accession were about to start, was a firmly committed European who gained Pompidou's confidence: Britain acceded, along with Denmark and Ireland, in 1973. After Heath lost the general election in 1974, British governments largely reverted to regarding the Community as a trading arrangement and hence opposed federal steps and, indeed, many policy developments that were not directly related to the Common Market. Their opposition was much less absolute than de Gaulle's had been; they were ready to bargain in order to secure decisions they favoured or more generally to remain as far as possible "at the heart of Europe." However, their methods were, as graphically described by a participant in a number of such negotiations, to result in delaying, weakening, blocking or opting out of what they saw as moves in a federal direction.[37]

Effective pressure for federal steps revived in 1974 when Valéry Giscard d'Estaing became French President and Helmut Schmidt German Chancellor. Giscard, after consultation with Monnet, proposed direct elections for the European Parliament, which had been already envisaged in the ECSC Treaty but required unanimous agreement.[38] The other member states agreed that they should be held in 1977 but the British, with the Labour government that succeeded Heath, insisted on "renegotiating" the terms of entry and subsequently holding a referendum on the result. This caused a delay until 1979. It was Roy Jenkins (a former Vice-Chairman of Federal Union), however, who as President of the Commission initiated the launching of monetary integration with the European Monetary System, which was backed by Schmidt and Giscard and also came into effect in 1979, as the first major step towards the common currency.

The two decisive federal steps of the late twentieth century came later when Jacques Delors was President of the Commission, Helmut Kohl German Chancellor and François Mitterrand French President. Delors consciously sought to follow the tradition of Monnet, Spinelli and Hallstein.[39] Seeking to identify, as Monnet had done, a decisive federal step which would attract the necessary support, he visited all the heads of government before taking up his post as President of the Commission in January 1981, to find out whether and which they would support out of what he saw as potentially decisive steps: single market, single currency, defence integration, institutional reform. All, including Mrs. Thatcher, who rejected the other options, said yes to the single market.

While this choice was consistent with the routine British view of the Community as a device for creating a market, Thatcher believed that the single market should be created, not through a treaty but by "gentlemen's agreement": a scarcely credible procedure for establishing the complex legislation that a modern market economy requires. She voted in the European Council against the proposal to convene an intergovernmental conference to draft such a treaty, but the proposal was adopted. She then demonstrated the better side of Britain's behaviour as a member state – respect for the rule of law. While unprecedented in the European Council, the majority vote was not unlawful. Margaret Thatcher's adviser on European Community affairs had discovered the advantage of having a copy of the treaty at hand. If it could be demonstrated that something she wanted to do would not be in accordance with the law, she would not do it. So Britain participated in the IGC and accepted many small federal steps, such as treaty amendment to provide for qualified majority voting for many single market measures, as part of the bargain to secure agreement on establishing an effective single market. Thatcher also made an important contribution by nominating the immensely able Lord Cockfield as Commissioner for internal market affairs. This embodied another fairly common characteristic of British people working in the institutions: that of accepting wholeheartedly what is needed to make the institutions work, which Cockfield did together with Delors - securing the adoption of nearly 300 legislative Acts required for the functioning of the single market.

The Single Act also contained quite a few of what Delors called "factors of progress," mainly smaller steps towards federal institutions or powers. These included, in addition to the provision for majority voting, without which the legislative programme would never have been enacted, the "co-operation procedure" giving the Parliament the beginnings of legislative codecision with the Council. As regards competences and powers, the initiation of environmental policy was promising as was the cohesion policy for aid to less-developed regions; and the aspiration of monetary union in the preamble, which Margaret Thatcher regarded as a rhetorical flourish, was in fact regarded as a serious commitment by most of the other member states.

Maastricht and the single currency

The dominance of the Deutsche Mark and the Bundesbank, giving Germany power over France at the heart of economic policy, had vexed the French since the 1960s. That was why, despite the commitment to monetary integration as part of the agreement on British accession among the six founder states, the discussion in the Council broke down. The French wanted to start with creation of the single currency whilst the Germans insisted that it be accompanied by a common macroeconomic policy requiring majority voting in the Council and a transfer of powers to the European Parliament, which Pompidou's Gaullist government had not been willing to accept.[40] However, the European Monetary System and the free movement of capital, together with other consequences of the successful Single European Act, gave Delors the opening to move towards the second of his strategic options: the single currency. Having served as President Mitterrand's Finance Minister he could assure himself that there would be French backing. The position of Chancellor Kohl was more difficult. His federalist conviction was profound enough to encompass the single currency; and Germans had seen steps towards shared government in the European Community in order to ensure a stable, peaceful "milieu" around them as a fundamental national interest.[41] But the single currency was the bitterest pill for most Germans to swallow, and in particular for the financial sector and the powerful Bundesbank itself. It was the opening for German unification following the fall of the Berlin Wall that gave Kohl his chance.

When asked in the early 1960s by Christopher Layton, who was then covering the European Community for *The Economist*, what would be the principal aims of his future political career, Kohl's response was the union of Europe and the unification of Germany, which may explain why he was ready to move so quickly to secure both the united Germany and the next major federal step for the European Union (as it was shortly to be called). For France, the link between the two aims was the acute urgency of the French desire for the single currency as an anchor for a more powerful united Germany at the heart of the new Europe together with the right of France, as one of the four occupying powers, to veto the unification; and this was the determining motive for Germans to accept the transfer of monetary sovereignty. The photograph of Kohl and Mitterrand holding hands in front of one of the vast cemeteries for the million French and Germans who had perished around Verdun in the First World War symbolised the existential character of this keystone of the Maastricht Treaty.

Thatcher was bitterly opposed to both German unification and monetary union. But she was unable to prevent the former, against the will of the United States as well as France and the Soviet Union; and she could not stop the latter if France and Germany, together with most of the other member states, were willing to accept the single currency without British participation. So the main objective of her successor, John Major, in the negotiations for the Maastricht Treaty was to secure agreement on a British opt-out from the single currency, in return for which he was ready to accept some federal steps such as more qualified majority voting (QMV) in the Council and a substantial introduction of legislative codecision for the Parliament - though not the use of the word "federal" to replace the open-ended "ever closer union" in the preamble. Thus the Maastricht Treaty established the European Union, with the two predominantly inter-governmental "pillars," for Common Foreign and Security Policy and for Justice and Home Affairs, alongside the existing, partly federal, European Community. The UK was committed to participate in the single currency eventually, but without any specific timescale.

Britain, Europe and New Labour

The last Labour Party Conference before New Labour's election victory in 1996 unanimously approved a statement of policy on the EU, emanating from a group containing the party's leading figures as well as senior MEPs and other experts. The statement contained policy proposals for the forthcoming intergovernmental conference, including extension of QMV in areas such as environmental, industrial and regional policy.[42] Tony Blair became Prime Minister just before the IGC in Amsterdam, where he impressed Britain's partners by accepting not only the Social Charter but also more QMV than Helmut Kohl, who was constrained by the constitutional powers of the Länder. Blair subsequently made some outstandingly pro-European speeches. However, he did this on the Continent, whilst those he delivered in the UK were notably more circumspect, doubtless partly because of potentially hostile reactions from the media, which could damage electoral prospects. A consequence was that, in the absence of a sufficiently authoritative presentation of the case for a constructive European policy, euroscepticism and europhobia flourished.

This deterioration in the political climate surrounding Britain's European policy accompanied the failure to hold the promised referendum on the euro, which reinforced doubts on the Continent as to whether the British would accept further deepening of the Union, such as had accompanied previous enlargements, to prevent its weakening as a result of the forthcoming enlargement to the east. Margaret Thatcher had after all made no secret of her hope that the enlargement would dilute the Union's supranational characteristics.[43] As there was not enough evidence of a radical break in the new government's policy in this respect and its stance on the euro continued to drift, the idea of a new initiative, perhaps on the part of a vanguard group of member states, became increasingly influential. Foreign Minister Joschka Fischer's advocacy of the formation of a group moving towards a federation within the Union, as a nucleus to attract the other member states to join them, was one example, which opened up discussion of, as he put it, the Union's federal finalité.[44] This was followed by the declaration attached to the Treaty of Nice opening the way to the constitutional convention, with terms of reference skilfully drafted by the Belgian Presidency of December 2002 to include the elements of federal reform as well as items that would enable the sceptics to approve the text.

Most of the participants in the convention that the European Council convened were parliamentarians; and most of them, including many of the MPs representing member states' parliaments, supported the more federalist proposals. Among the governments' representatives there were several with similar views, but also a number of intergovernmentalists, led by the British, who resisted most of the federal elements. Giscard d'Estaing presided with great skill, to reach his preferred outcome of pleasing the majority of parliamentarians and some governments with more federal institutions for matters such as the single market, while satisfying the more sceptical, including particularly the British, with a basically intergovernmental structure for the commanding heights of macroeconomic policy and of foreign policy and defence. This succeeded brilliantly in securing the unanimous approval of the European Council and hence the signatures on the constitutional treaty of the authorised representatives of all 25 member states, followed by ratification by 16 of them. But in order to keep the subject out of the polemics surrounding the elections to the European Parliament, Blair had decided to put it to a referendum. President Chirac then felt obliged to do the same, as did the Dutch; and following their voters' "no," the British government lost no time in manifesting its relief.

Acceptance of the text by parliamentarians and governments, followed by rejection by French and Dutch voters, may be due partly to the nature of the document: its text more suitable to politicians and officials than to voters. However, there were doubtless also more fundamental causes. Previous major institutional reforms had been accompanied by major projects, such as the common market, the single market and the single currency, each combined with the consolidation of peaceful relations among the member states. The constitutional treaty was intended to respond to the challenge of incorporating eight new Central and East European states. However, by the time of the referendums, this was already a fait accompli, not welcome to many of those who voted no, particularly in France. Whilst security and prosperity had been important motives for preceding reforms, moreover, they may well be more salient conditions when citizens' assent in referendums is required. So the problem of securing the support of the sceptical British may be of more general relevance than hitherto.

The British, security, climate change and defence

The story of Britain and the European Union, from the Community's earliest days in the form of the ECSC until today, clearly demonstrates that the British have not envisaged the developing Union as a framework which, by permanently guaranteeing pacific relations among the member states, would contribute greatly to their security. By way of contrast, many in the founding states, including key political leaders, have been acutely conscious of that motive. This has induced them to initiate or accept, with generally satisfactory results, the radical reform of moving towards shared, federal government in fields where cross-frontier forces have made self-government by member states no longer adequate. It is misguided to argue that, because war among member states is no longer conceivable, the institutions have served their purpose and the federal elements need no further development, or are even no longer required. The growth of cross-frontier influences, on security and the economy in particular, is a consequence of technological development, which will not go away. Application of federal principles will become more necessary, not less. As far as internal security and prosperity are concerned, the Union still has much to do in order to ensure that it is fully effective and democratic; and its governance falls very far short of dealing effectively with the influences that cross its external frontiers. It is here, in the relations with the wider world outside, that the application of federal principles is most damagingly inadequate.

Since the mid-1960s the Community has been the equal of the United States in trade negotiations, with its federal element of the Commission as its negotiator, responsible to the Council backed by provision for qualified majority voting, and using a federal instrument in the form of the common external tariff.[45] The consequence has been, for all the evident shortcomings, a massive reduction of tariffs during the past four decades and the introduction of a more effective rule of law within the World Trade Organisation than exists in any other field of international relations. However, although the Union could have a similar benign effect in other fields of international relations, thus helping to make the world around it safer and more prosperous, it has generally lacked the vision and the will to equip itself with the necessary powers and institutions.

It was particularly encouraging that the EU played the leading part in securing agreement on the Kyoto Protocol, with the British Presidency of the Council during the crucial concluding negotiation: the Union subsequently used the instrument of its trade policy to obtain the Russian ratification that was required to enable the Protocol to enter into force. Although this is only a first step towards preventing what could otherwise be catastrophic climate change, it demonstrates the Union's capacity to make the leading contribution to averting what may be the greatest danger facing mankind. It is noteworthy that the British part in the Union's performance has not been subjected to much criticism, even by eurosceptics, save when Blair appeared, following the G8 summit under British Presidency at Gleneagles in 2005, to qualify his support for further development of the Kyoto principle by offering comfort to President Bush's preference for supporting technological development as an adequate substitute. Blair's support for the Union's policy of cutting carbon emissions by 60 per cent by mid-century has not been subject to widespread criticism.

Another of Blair's initiatives for developing the Union's role in the world was his agreement with President Chirac to support the principle of an EU rapid reaction force for peace-keeping and peace-making, which is in a somewhat prolonged process of development, leading to other forms of common military action with similar aims. This British contribution to ending the inhibition against common European activity in the field of defence, which had lasted for nearly half a century after the collapse of the European Defence Community, was also subjected to remarkably little criticism in Britain, save by those who rejected any role beyond compliance with the wishes of the United States. This is less surprising than it may seem, given that eurobarometer surveys have consistently shown that a role for the Union in the field of defence has strong support among the British.

Evidently British participation in these policies that began to strengthen the Union's role in promoting security in the wider world did not evoke the kneejerk hostile reactions so often evoked by proposals for strengthening common action within the Union itself.

Europe in the world: the last frontier for Britain and a federal Europe

With the common market, the single market and the single currency, and associated institutional reforms, the Union has taken major steps towards a shared federal governance of the cross-frontier economic relationships among member states. Given the general failure of the British to appreciate the Union's significance in contributing to their security, the fear of economic loss through exclusion from its development has been the principal motive so far for British participation in accepting federal steps; and this lack of positive motivation will, so long as it lasts, doubtless remain an obstacle in the way of action that will be needed even to maintain, let alone strengthen, the Union's effectiveness with the enlarged and still enlarging membership.

One consequence could be a possibly terminal decline in the Union's effectiveness. A second could be that other member states, based on the eurozone or a smaller group, would press ahead with further steps of integration, perhaps leading the British to join them. A third could follow from British understanding that the Union could make a major contribution towards creating a safer world, which remains a vast field in which its potential has not been realised. The Union could be at least the equal of the United States, not only in the world trading system where it has since the 1960s made an indispensable contribution to liberal trade and an international rule of law, but also in most fields other than the military.

The euro is already a heavyweight currency in money and capital markets, but the US still dominates the international monetary system. With a common negotiator backed by provision for majority voting among the ministers of eurozone states, however, the euro could have a decisive stabilising impact on the international system, which in the absence of a countervailing monetary power is vulnerable to violent shifts in interest and exchange rates generated by events in the US economy. The EU and member states together provide four times as much aid and assistance as the US, largely for mainstream purposes of action in favour of economic development and against poverty and disease. But the Union is also better placed than the US in helping to build structures for good governance, which is surely at least as necessary for people's general welfare in many countries as mainstream development aid. A combination of effective policies in such fields, along with a significant and growing capacity for peace-keeping and peace-making, would be an essential complement to preponderant military power and could be a crucial contribution to making the world a safer place for its people.

Climate change is almost certainly a greater threat to the security of mankind than any with which military power can deal; and the EU has, with the Kyoto Protocol, already shown its capacity for leading the world towards an effective remedy. However, this is only a first step towards cutting carbon emissions by over half by the middle of this century, which leading scientists regard as essential and which is the aim of the EU's policy. A successful initiative by the Union to lead a group of states from both North and South of the world in forming a vanguard community committed to go beyond Kyoto with a radical policy to this end would have great potential.[46] Such a community could confront the danger of climate change by limiting carbon emissions and promoting sustainable development among the participating states, offering association with partial measures to those not ready to become full members, with the ultimate objective of universal membership. For the Union to perform this leading role in an effective and democratic way, the member states would need to accept majority voting in the Council, codecision with the European Parliament and a strong role for the Commission in the relevant policy fields. Whereas resistance to federal steps of military integration has proved hard to overcome, integration on federal lines to avert intolerable climate change should not encounter such deeply rooted opposition.

The descent of Europe during the past century from being the home of great world powers to dependence on the Americans has diverted the attention of too many Europeans from fundamental realities of geopolitics which make it urgent that the Union exert a more powerful influence on the global system. The United States, as for the time being the world's only superpower, is unable to ensure security. China is on course to become another before very long. But there is not much awareness of the danger of a world dominated by what are likely to remain two superpowers with radically different political cultures; and while the perception is growing that India may later be added to the list, the potential for the European Union to become much more rapidly a really great power, with pre-eminence in a number of fields despite lesser military might, is barely recognised.

Europeans, given their stage of historical development and consequent preference for multilateral arrangements in the wider world, together with an aptitude derived from their experience of sharing governance in the Community and Union, are uniquely qualified to lead the world in the direction of shared government. The completion of such a process may well take a century or more. The European Community has, after all, taken over half a century to become the Union of today. But the relationships among member states changed for the better soon after the process of building a federal democracy together began; wars between them became unthinkable; they learnt to co-operate closely in new fields; and the merits of membership led others to join so that the Union now contains the majority of European states.

This chapter has sought to show that a root cause of the British refusal to support developments towards a federal Europe has been the failure to associate them with the benefits of security rather than of economic advantage alone; and this may also be a cause of a loss of enthusiasm for further development of the Union in other member states. Making the European Union a prime mover for improving security in the wider world would be a proper application of federal principle which could restore dynamism to the Union's development. Better understanding of this contribution to security in Europe and the world could also help the British to understand the merits of federal principles, and perhaps to recover the enthusiasm for the idea which they supported so remarkably as the way to replace the perilous international anarchy that led to World War Two.

★ ★ ★

The Lisbon Treaty, which was signed by all member states shortly before this book went to press, embodies a set of reforms designed to make the Union more democratic and effective. Democracy is to be enhanced by making codecision of the Parliament and the Council the normal legislative procedure; by eliminating the holding of closed sessions by the Council when acting as a legislative chamber; and by requiring the European Council to take account of the results of the European elections when nominating the Commission's Presidents, who must be approved by the Parliament. Government of the Union is to be made more effective, with qualified majority as the Council's normal legislative procedure; with the European Council electing its Presidents not for a six-month but for a thirty-month term renewable once, during which time he or she is not to be distracted by holding any national office; and with the number of Commissioners cut by one-third.

A further set of reforms is designed to strengthen the Union's ability to safeguard European interests and to make its due contribution to prosperity and security in the world as a whole. The High Representative for Foreign Affairs and Security is to be appointed by the European Council to coordinate the Union's external role across the board, combining Chairmanship of the Council of Foreign Ministers and of the Political and Security Committee with, as a Vice-President of the Commission, oversight of the full range of its external responsibilities. The Treaty also provides more clearly for external action on climate change and energy solidarity and, in the field of defence, for a group of willing member states to establish 'permanent structured co-operation'.

The Treaty appears likely to be ratified; and, if it is not, past experience indicates that either the member states will find it necessary to adopt many of its provisions, or a group of them will, as with the euro, go ahead without waiting for the rest. It is particularly important for British people to appreciate that this Treaty will enable the Union not only to function better internally, but also to move further towards realising its full potential to help make the world a safer and more prosperous place.

We have a new opportunity to apply, in a practical and beneficial way, the thinking behind the federal principles to which British people have in the past, as this book has shown, made such a notable contribution.

Notes to Chapter 8

[1] An authoritative analysis of the position of the American founding fathers is to be found in Maurice J.C. Vile, *The Structure of American Federalism* (Oxford: Oxford University Press, 1961).

[2] Alexis de Tocqueville, *De la Démocratie en Amérique* (Paris, 1835); in English as *Democracy in America*, G. Lawrence (ed.), (London: Fontana Press, 1994); Michael Burgess, *Comparative Federalism: Theory and Practice* (London: Routledge, 2006), ch. 3, passim; John Pinder, 'Federalism and the British Liberal Tradition', in Andrea Bosco (ed.), *The Federal Idea. Vol. 1, The History of federalism from the Enlightenment to 1945* (London: Lothian Foundation Press, 1991), pp.99-118.

[3] James Bryce, *The American Commonwealth* (London: Macmillan, 1919; 1st edn New York, 1888).

[4] cf Michael Burgess, *Comparative Federalism*, pp. 105-7, and *The British Tradition of Federalism* (London: Cassell, 1995), pp.100-01; see also Pinder, *op.cit.*, pp. 102-3.

[5] Sir John R. Seeley, *The Expansion of England* (London: 1883; 2nd edn., 1895); Burgess, *The British Tradition of Federalism*, pp. 133-4; and Pinder, *ibid.*, pp. 108-9.

[6] John Seeley, 'United States of Europe', *MacMillans Magazine*, Vol. 23, March 1871, pp. 436- 48; see Burgess, *The British Tradition of Federalism*, *loc.cit.*, and Pinder, *loc.cit.*

[7] See Walter Lipgens, 'General Introduction', pp. 1-5, and John Pinder, Introduction to ch. l, 'Federal Union 1939-41', pp. 26-34, in Walter Lipgens (ed.), *Documents on the History of European Integration, Vol. 2: Plans for European Union in Great Britain and in Exile 1939-1945* (Berlin and New York: de Gruyter, 1986); and Richard Mayne and John Pinder, *Federal Union: The Pioneers - A History of Federal Union* (Basingstoke: Macmillan, 1990), ch. 1-3.

[8] Mayne and Pinder, *ibid.*, p. 28.

[9] Winston S. Churchill, *The Second World War,* Vol.2 (London: Cassell, 1948), pp. 180-1.

[10] Sir John Colville, *The Fringes of Power: Downing Street Diaries 1939-1955* (London: Hodder &Stoughton, 1985), p. 161.

[11] W.B. Curry, *The Case for Federal Union* (Harmondsworth: Penguin Special, 1939).

12 Clarence K. Streit, *Union Now: A Proposal for a Federal Union of the Democracies of the North Atlantic* (London and New York: Jonathan Cape and Harper, 1939).

13 Lord Lothian (Philip Kerr), *Pacifism is not Enough, nor Patriotism Either* (OUP 1935); reprinted in *Pacifism is not Enough: Collected Lectures and Speeches of Lord Lothian (Philip Kerr)*, edited by John Pinder and Andrea Bosco (London and New York: Lothian Foundation Press, 1990).

14 For example, W. Ivor Jennings, *A Federation for Western Europe* (Cambridge University Press, 1940); R.W.G. Mackay, *Federal Europe* (London: Michael Joseph, 1940), both containing draft constitutions.

15 Lionel Robbins, *National Planning, and International Order* (London: Macmillan, 1937).

16 Lionel Robbins, *The Economic Causes of War* (London: Jonathan Cape, 1939), ch. 5 and p. 109.

17 Daniel J. Elazar, *Exploring Federalism* (Tuscaloosa: University of Alabama Press, 1987), p. 12.

18 Altiero Spinelli, *Come ho tentato di diventare saggio: Io, Ulisse* (Bologna: Il Mulino, 1984), pp. 307-8; English translation of this passage in Mayne and Pinder, *op.cit.*, p. 84.

19 See Altiero Spinelli and Emesto Rossi, *Il Manifesto di Ventotene* (Milano: Oscar Mondadori, 2006; 1st edn. Rome, 1944).

20 Etienne Hirsch, *Ainsi va la vie* (Lausanne: Fondation Jean Monnet pour l'Europe), p. 222.

21 Declaration by Robert Schuman, French Foreign Minister, 9 May 1950.

22 Cited in Jeremy Moon, *European Integration in British Politics: A Study of Issue Change* (Aldershot: Gower, 1985), p. 5.

23 Alexander Hamilton, John Jay, James Madison, *The Federalist*; Louis Joxe, 'Contribution', in Henri Rieben, *Des Guerres Européennes à l'Union de l'Europe* (Lausanne: Fondation Jean Monnet pour l'Europe, 2004), pp. 252-3; information from a senior official in the High Authority.

24 Walter Lipgens (ed.), *45 Jahre Ringen über die Europäische Verfassung* (Bonn: Europa Union Verlag, 1986), pp. 304-6.

25 Winston S. Churchill, Speech in Zurich on 19 September 1946, reproduced in Walter Lipgens and Wilfried Loth (eds), *Documents on the History of European Integration, Vol.3, The Struggle for European Union by Political Parties and Pressure Groups in Western European Countries 1945-1950* (Berlin and New York: de Gruyter, 1988), pp. 664-5.

26 Mayne and Pinder, *op.cit.*, p. 120.

[27] For example Ernst B. Haas, *The Uniting, of Europe: Political, Social and Economical Forces, 1950-1957* (London: Stevens, 1958); Leon N. Lindberg, *The Political Dynamics of European Economic Integration* (Stanford, Cal.: Stanford University Press, 1963); Leon N. Lindberg and Stuart A. Scheingold, *Europe's Would-be Polity: Patterns of Change in the European Community* (Inglewood Cliffs, N.J.: Prentice-Hall, 1970).

[28] Alan Milward, *The Reconstruction of Western Europe 1954-51* (London: Methuen, 1984), pp. 129,137.

[29] Alan Milward, *The European Rescue of the Nation-State* (London: Routledge, 1992), p. 435.

[30] Jean Monnet, *Memoirs* (London: William Collins, 1978), p. 343.

[31] Henri Rieben, Claire Camperio and Françoise Nicoud (eds), *A l'Ecoute de Jean Monnet* (Lausanne: Fondation Jean Monnet pour l'Europe, 2004), pp. 97-8.

[32] Luigi Majocchi and Francesco Rossolillo, *Il Parlamento Europeo* (Napoli: Guida Editori, 1979), pp. 47-9, 179-99.

[33] Altiero Spinelli, *Diario europeo 1948-1969*, edited by Edmondo Paolini (Bologna: Il Mulino, 1989), p. 84.

[34] *ibid.*, pp. 137-8.

[35] *ibid.*, pp. 170-1.

[36] Mayne and Pinder, *op.cit.*, p. 106; Paul-Henri Spaak, *The Continuing Battle: Memoirs of a European 1936-66* (London: Weidenfeld and Nicholson, 1971), p. 217.

[37] Tommaso Padoa-Schioppa, *Europe: A Civil Power* (London: Federal Trust, 2004), pp. 82-4.

[38] François Duchêne, *Jean Monnet: The First Statesman of Interdependence* (New York and London: W. W. Norton, 1994), pp. 336-7.

[39] Jacques Delors, *Mémoires* (Paris: Plon, 2004), p. 175.

[40] Loukas Tsoukalis, *The Politics and Economics of European Monetary Integration* (London: Oxford University Press, 1977), pp. 88-9.

[41] Simon Bulmer, Charlie Jeffery and William E. Patterson, *Germany's European Diplomacy: Shaping the regional milieu* (Manchester: Manchester University Press, 2000).

[42] 'The future of the European Union: Report on Labour's position in preparation for the Intergovernmental Conference 1996', approved by the Party Conference October 1995 (London: Labour Party, 1995).

[43] Margaret Thatcher, *The Downing Street Years* (London: HarperCollins, 1993), ch. 16.

44 Joschka Fischer, *From Confederation to Federation: Thoughts on the Finality of European Integration,* European Essay No.8 (London: Federal Trust, 2000), pp. 16-24.

45 Lawrence B. Krause, *European Economic Integration and the United States* (Washington, D.C.: The Brookings Institution, 1968), p. 224-5.

46 This was suggested in John Pinder, 'The Rule of Law for a Uniting World: A Global Community for Sustainable Development', in Willem J.M. van Genugten *et al.* (eds), *Realism and Moralism in International Relations* (The Hague: Kluwer Law International, 1999), pp. 149-67. The policy of Action for a Global Climate Community is similar.

Biographical Notes on Contributors

Michael Burgess is Professor, and Director of the Centre for Federal Studies, at the University of Kent. He is co-ordinator of Kent's MA in Comparative Federalism. The leading authority on the history of federalism in Britain, his published books include *The British Tradition of Federalism* and *Comparative Federalism: theory and practice*.

Richard Corbett is a Member of the European Parliament representing Yorkshire and Humber. He is Deputy Leader of the group of Labour MEPs and spokesman on constitutional affairs for the Socialist Group. He is joint author of the standard textbook on the European Parliament which is now in its seventh edition.

Brendan Donnelly is Director of the Federal Trust. He worked for the Foreign Office, the European Parliament and the Commission before serving as a Member of the European Parliament from 1994 to 1999. He is Chairman of Federal Union and author of numerous research papers on contemporary developments in the European Union.

Stanley Henig was Professor of European Politics at the University of Central Lancashire. He was a Member of Parliament from 1966 to 1970 and later Leader of Lancaster City Council. A Senior Research Fellow at Federal Trust, he headed the "Federal Britain" project. He is author of nine books on British and European politics.

Lucio Levi is Professor of Political Science and Comparative Politics at the University of Turin. He is a member of the executive committee of the World Federalist Movement and of the Federal Committee of the Union of European Federalists. He edits *The Federalist Debate* and is author of various books on federalism, European integration and international organisations.

Richard Mayne worked with Jean Monnet for many years and also translated his memoirs into English (winning the Scott-Moncrieff prize). As a senior official of the European Commission, he was for a time personal assistant to Walter Hallstein, the first President. A former co-editor of *Encounter*, his published books include *The Recovery of Europe* and (with John Pinder) *Federal Union: the Pioneers*.

John Palmer is a member of the Governing Board of the European Policy Centre (EPC) – a Brussels-based think tank (www.theepc.be). He was Political Director of the EPC from 1996 to 2005. Previously he was European editor of *The Guardian*.

John Pinder was Director of the Policy Studies Institute and is Honorary Professor at the College of Europe. He is a former Vice-President of the International European Movement, President of the Union of European Federalists and Chairman of the Federal Trust. He is author of several books on European integration and federalism.

Maurice Vile was Professor of Political Science and Deputy Vice Chancellor of the University of Kent. From 1989 to 1994 he was Director of British programmes for Boston University; he has been a Visiting Professor at a number of American universities. Widely acknowledged as a world authority on American federalism, he is author of books and articles on the constitution and politics of the US.

Ernest Wistrich was Director of the European Movement (UK) from 1969 to 1986. He organised and led the campaigns for British membership of the European Community, for a "yes" vote in the 1975 referendum and against withdrawal in 1982-3.